Champions Break Chains

Champions Break Chains

Dr. Chandra Gill

Foreword by Dr. Julianne Malveaux

Blackademically Speaking Enterprises

Chicago, IL

Blackademically Speaking Enterprises
PO Box 803468
Chicago, IL 60680-3468

Champions Break Chains
by Dr. Chandra Gill
Foreword by Dr. Julianne Malveaux

First Edition Paperback
Printed in the United States of America

Edited by Elliot Bratton
Book layout and design by Borel Graphics
Cover art by istock.com and gettyimages.com
Inside Photography by Jamel Shabazz

ISBN 978-0-9829863-0-1
African-American Studies | Education | United States History | Social Justice
Non-fiction

Visit our website at www.drchandragill.com

DEDICATION

This book is dedicated to the memory of my daddy, Maurice Gill, Jr.
April 14, 1951 - June 22, 2010

Daddy, I love you forever
I am because of YOU!
I can forget you Never
Your wisdom will hold true:

"There was a time I heard every word our Lord spoke to me. Being young and foolish I closed my ears to Him. My sight of Him became dim. At one time I thought He had forsaken me. I always thought something was blocking my view. Over time I stopped looking around and down. I looked up. My Lord Jesus Christ was blocking my sight. He stated I have always been here for you, ask and you will receive. Through your lives, Dr. Chandra Nicole Gill and your brother Marcus Gill, He has granted my request. Paying forward and asking others to reciprocate are my thoughts and wishes. Stay true to your life, there is more to come. Dad"

From: mauricegill@vzw.blackberry.net
Saturday, May 1, 2010 at 7:19 PM

Champions Break Chains is dedicated to YOU!

ACKNOWLEDGMENTS

His name was Marshall McMillan. He owned pigs. He received a visit from a group of White men, who demanded to have his pigs. They offered to buy them. He refused to sell them. They shot him; they killed him. The issue? Pigs. It's fair to say that he was murdered in exchange for his convictions.

Marshall McMillan was my great-great-grandfather. I am inspired daily by the people of my own ancestral bloodline and their strength. I have been abundantly blessed in learning of my genealogy, for I know courage and conviction flow through my veins. My great-uncle, Dezzie B, is 92 years of age. I am blessed by his presence and his memory as he shares our story, our history as a family. I am grateful for our elder, Lonnie Gill, a distant cousin who is 96 years of age.

As I ponder the strength and resilience of my bloodline, I am quick to give God the glory! I then give my overwhelmingly incredible parents the credit. My father, Maurice Gill, worked hard every day and all day. As a sound provider, he blessed me and my life's chances. My mother, Cheryl Ann Gill, is the greatest woman that I know, period! She worked even harder (imagine that) and she sacrificed oh so much, which in turn blessed my life's choices.

I am grateful for my brother, Marcus Gill (and Angel). His courage to stand up and be strong is admirable. He beat the streets of Chicago and will go down in history as one of Woodlawn's finest blackademicians ever—from the streets to the suites.

I am indebted to both of my grandmothers (Louise Ellis & Valorita Boles), each of whom turned 75 years old in 2010—what a blessing! I live, love and laugh in memory of my granddaddy, Maurice Gill, who only experienced his desired educational experience through me.

For years, I was referenced as a first-generation college student within my family unit. The eventual academic accomplishment of obtaining my Ph.D. thus made me a "first" all over again. Then I learned more of my history that suggested otherwise. I appreciate yet another elder (maternal) in my family, Turner Battle. His research of our family dates back to the 18th century. I am honored to know much of my story.

This book is a deposit into the spiritual accounts of my unborn children and their future. It is written for my favorite lil' people, my niece (Marlicia), my nephew (Marcus) and my God-daughter (Iman). It is hopeful motivation for my God-son whom I just reconnected with, Davontae, a first-year college student. I love each of you! It is written in memory of Demetrius Jones and Anita Terrell, two of the most significant college friendships ever experienced. No words can describe what each of you offered me in your short time on earth. In memory of my little buddy, Nailah Franklin, who left us oh so soon; God knows all!

In honor of my many aunties, uncles, and cousins, I say thank you. I love my family with a perfecting love that grows each and every day. To my extended family, my great friends, Kandria, Walidah, Manvel, Tanya, Joy, and Edna Lee Moffitt, thanks for being there through the writing and reading of this book. To one of my best friends, a very special man, Dr. Roderic Land—I say thank you. I love each of you.

I thank each of my friends, Tami, Dani, Misty, Renee, Yogi, Freddie B, JP, (far too many to name). I thank the women of Delta Sigma Theta Sorority, Inc. for the extraordinary work and sacrifice offered unto the world, in changing the world—specifically Alpha Nu Chapter, my initiating chapter, and Theta Zeta alongside Chicago Alumnae Chapter. I must acknowledge where it all began: my Woodlawn, Andrew Carnegie and Lindblom family–*Swoop!*

A special thanks is offered to my legal team, Atty. Lewis Myers, Atty. Berve Power and Atty. Warren Ballentine in their fight for my freedom. I thank Atty. Paul Langer and Atty. Doressia Hutton for their legal assistance with my pardon. I'm grateful to State Representative Connie Howard, Congressman Danny Davis, Reverend Jesse Jackson and Dr. James Anderson for their statements in support of my character, thus my pardon. I give thanks to Savitri, India, Geovanda, Aaron, LaTasha, Dr. Carol Adams, Gary Flowers, John Mitchell, Eddie Read, Rev. James Meeks and Dr. Julianne Malveaux for their unwavering fight for justice.

I concede always to the amazing intellect of my academic advisory team, Dr. Laurence Parker, Dr. William Trent, Dr. David Stovall, Dr. Christopher Spann and Dr. Norman K. Denzin. On behalf of the most awesome scholarship family around, the Gates Millennium Scholars, I say watch out; we're going to change the world. Thanks, Mary and Larry for your incredible leadership with our delicate minds and careers. Thank you Bishop and Mama Gwin. Thanks to Tara, Miyoshi, Tina, Rashada and Demetrius for your love, support and thoughts.

Many thanks to my publishing team: my editor, Elliot Bratton (what a beginning); my graphic designer, Denise Billups of Borel Graphics; Toussaint Werner, my graphics artist; Patrick Oliver, the book wiz; and Brother Jamel Shabazz for his uniquely captured photographic images. Finally, a premier thank you to Nenad and Dr. Webber for their well-informed approaches to healing. You are an invaluable asset to my work personally, professionally and spiritually.

TABLE OF CONTENTS

FOREWORD

by Dr. Julianne Malveaux

D r. Chandra Gill is a champion. She is absolutely passionate about motivating African American people to embrace education and says she wants to "properly educate, powerfully motivate and persistently graduate our children, and again our people." She challenges people with both simple and profound questions. Why haven't you finished that GED? What are you doing with your life? Why aren't you doing more? And because she is anointed, she challenges black people from a profoundly spiritual place with an eloquence that encompasses both academic eloquence and street talk.

Gill has impeccable academic credentials. Armed with a Ph.D. in Educational Policy Studies from the University of Illinois, with the distinction of being in the first class of Gates Millennium Scholars, she has both held conventional academic positions and attracted a large popular following. Her radio program and her company, Blackademically Speaking, reflect her commitment to "make it plain", or to make knowledge accessible.

I met Chandra Gill in 2005 when I spent a week at the University of Illinois in Urbana as a visiting faculty member. When we talked, she shared the incongruous story of her encounter with the law and her felony conviction. I found it impossible to believe that this petite young woman was accused of "choking" a burly off-duty police officer that may not have identified himself as such until it was too late. I also found it unfathomable that a young sister, in the course of doing community service by mentoring girls, could have been so brutally mishandled by the criminal "just us" system. Ultimately, Chandra was blessedly pardoned from her felony conviction, but how many who are mishandled and misjudged are not pardoned?

In *Champions Break Chains,* Dr. Gill turns her attention to those who have had the misfortune of a collision with law "enforcement" and also have not had her advantages. In doing so, she is an inheritor of Ida B. Wells, and WEB DuBois. Wells, the trailblazing journalist who chronicled discrimination and lynching, was a vocal critic of the status quo, both inside and outside the African American community. DuBois, our pre-eminent scholar, combined scholarship and activism for the betterment of African American people.

Writing for her own hip-hop generation, Chandra has compiled a set of short pieces that are provocative, inspirational, motivational, and educational. She writes about black history, black religion, the black family, black money and black leadership. Almost every essay contains a challenge, though her tone alternates from fiery to gentle, depending on the subject matter. Her clear goal – to get people reading, thinking and changing.

The spirituality implicit in this work is important to recognize. During a recent appearance at Bennett College for Women, Chandra was able to touch students profoundly, effortlessly moving from lecture mode to preacher mode, and ending her powerful talk with an "altar call" that brought most students to the front of the Annie Merner Pfeiffer Chapel to pray. This same seamless switch from motivational writing to preaching is evident in this writing, an important feature of this work.

Dr. Chandra Gill is a woman to watch. The combination of her academic acumen, spiritual anointing, passionate commitment to education, and ardent embrace of the African American community have placed her on an important and transformative path. After reading *Champions Break Chains,* I await her next contribution to the public dialogue.

—Julianne Malveaux, Ph.D.

President, Bennett College for Women

Greensboro, North Carolina

INTRODUCTION

by Dr. Chandra Gill

Black people are resilient, beautiful and purely genius. We have a running history of victory in America and we are largely responsible for the greatness seen throughout the world. Simply put, we know how to overcome. So why are we seemingly married to mediocrity and mistakenly excited about damaging excuses in life? If we are to all see the very change we so desire, our communities must accept individual responsibility as a core virtue and our country must acknowledge institutional accountability as a significant part of the cure. Yes, our children are our future, but most important we are our children's future.

Over and over again we read about the less than positive realities surrounding Black folks in this country. We are inundated with imagery on television and in videos that insist on portraying us as negative, ignorant, poor and even wicked. Sadly, much of this stereotypical imagery has been labeled entertainment, thus supported by our very own. Black folk who once ran away from plantations of evil in search of freedom now in wonderment stare down a generation of Black folk who voluntarily sing and dance on modern day plantations to the tune of their own enslavement. Are they clueless to who they really are?

Amazingly, the steaming effect of this behavior generates much dialogue and questions regarding Black folk in America. What remains interesting is a lack of responsibility and accountability amongst Americans in general. It is simply irresponsible to continually discuss the problems of Black America void of the evils that gave birth to such. Likewise, it is equally important for us to offer more than mere conversation regarding our issues; it is now time to best understand these issues historically with courageous acts in changing our own predicament.

All too often in connecting today's issues within the Black communities to slavery there is an astounding resistance. Black and White folk alike have conveniently dismissed such connections and continue to dilute the harsh impact slavery has had on Black folk. Furthermore, the complexities surrounding those who take inventory within our culture insists that we accept personal responsibility for ourselves. This is widely known as "airing our dirty laundry." This "dirty laundry" reference is directed at those who offer a critique of our culture publicly. It is when someone exposes family business to the general public. This book, however, is not about airing our "dirty laundry." From my personal standpoint, it is obvious that the laundry is dirty and it is time we clean it! While many insist on believing that our issues as Black folk in this country are our issues alone, the truth is America is in need of a deep cleaning from its greed, hate, evil and dominance. Black issues are either the byproduct of these realities or a mere microcosm of such.

Specific to our communities however, are damaging issues that are of no secret. Drive-by shootings, crack-cocaine, dilapidated schools, abandoned buildings, vacant lots and vacant thinking all challenge our communities. Here, such issues are classified as chains. These chains are identified with the bondage they create and even the thinking that account for them. This mental bondage is connected to thinking that is uncritical and disastrous. History points us to how Blacks were held captive by overseers, enslaved and chained to the plantations' evil. The results are seen today in the minds and actions of so many who unnaturally accept dead-end behaviors.

As we acknowledge that all of our laundry is not dirty, we must critically evaluate how these problems within inner city communities in particular, pose threats to our children unlike never before. When driving through our communities you cannot help but notice a spirit of powerlessness and hopelessness. Education for far too many of our youth occurs on street corners as opposed to strict classrooms. At early ages, our children are forced to navigate harsh realities such as the avoidance of gangs, drugs and severe violence. Furthering these challenges for our children are their parents who remain stuck in their own pain and unable to see a bright, healthy future. "Baby mama drama" and imprisoned fathers plague our communities at all time highs. Such hopeless situations account for hopeless spirits in people. Children in these environments are asked each day to be great despite the lack of greatness in their homes, communities and schools.

It is time to encourage motivation with education. From where I sit, it is a great challenge for anyone to succeed in education with a lack of motivation. Whereas it sounds fabulous to demand that our children work hard for their own education, truth is this: far too many live in environments that drain their motivation to achieve this so-called good education. It is simply irresponsible to speak for our children and their education without a framework of motivation that takes into account their dire and desperate needs. In other words, true education is indeed vital to the development of any people.

Yet this education for many Blacks in inner city communities is threatened when simply walking en route to the school building. One's social environment chokes your chances of ever breathing the school's hallways and cafeterias, let alone benefiting from a healthy learning experience. Our children are in need of motivation concerning their environment socially, simultaneous to schools that condone such educationally. This understanding amongst teachers, parents, policy-makers, politicians and administrators is mandatory as it creates a culture of relevance for Black students; it is this culture of relevance that will provide authentic opportunity for our children, best mirroring their heritage of excellence and genius.

When the world renown Michael Jackson wrote songs and danced, so did the world. When Muhammad Ali courageously defeated his opponents, the world watched and cheered. When Oprah Winfrey speaks to issues, people throughout the world endeavor to change the issues in their lives. From the Williams sisters of tennis, to Michael Jordan of basketball, to Tiger gracing the plains, African-Americans elegantly polish the planet as champions.

Often the questions are asked, "How did you make it out, Dr. Gill? How did you break the chains within your community only to emerge as the Ph.D. you are today? Surely you made good decisions, right?" I admit that decisions are important, as we will discuss here. I also admit that I am the woman I am today because of two loving human beings who were willing to be responsible parents. I contend however, that despite my few accomplishments in life, the challenges have at times been debatably unbearable and even unbelievable. Such is the story for many more inner-city youth. Unfortunately their struggle is far more paramount, leaving them as lifetime victims of realities they seem to never overcome:

> It's a warm sunny day outside and this day like many others
> welcomed our creativity in finding "something to do." In
> a community where liquor stores and churches dominated
> the blocks, there seemed to be little desire to build

community centers and recreational areas. Libraries and safe parks were as scarce as good schools with updated materials. So on this day, a beautiful summer day in Chicago, loud music dominated the airwaves as shooting dice and pitching pennies kept the older guys occupied. As for us, the younger ones, we were forced to also create fun activities, as is the case when there is really nothing to do. As with most of the other days, this included "hopping the tracks" or playing basketball on a makeshift rim nailed to the tree. So much for Jesus' story in being nailed to the cross because surely these nails were of great benefit in saving and keeping many focused on something constructive and trouble-free. Each summer in the 'hood was prophesied as a bloody summer: "This year is just gon' be a real bloody summer." This was echoed amongst many of those bearing witness to deaths during the school year and realizing that only as the weather got better, more deaths would come.

I had to be maybe nine or ten years old the very first time witnessing such behavior. Nonetheless, there were about five of us walking across the street where our grammar school was located this warm, sunny day. We witnessed a police car pull behind the school neighboring the nearby railroad tracks. We wondered why he would just park in a secluded area where no one was. Maybe he awaited a crime? Maybe this was a newly developed crime area void of the presence of people? Were there rapes we knew nothing about in this dense area behind the school...our school? After watching for maybe ten minutes, I surmise, we soon saw another head in the car. In laughter, we knew that this was yet another situation or, shall I say, a violation. See, this officer was like those we bore witness to several times before. Within a matter of seconds we witnessed this one head again. There was one head, then two. This game played out for some time, but this was no game!

What happens in a community where those called to "serve and protect" sometimes serve only their desires in protection of their own interests? How does a child prosper in such an environment? Surely, the mantra of "I am not a role model" is real for many but aren't police officers and teachers and firemen merely local working citizens bearing the 'role model' label?

It wasn't long before we concluded that the police officers were using the dense and secluded area as a space to themselves commit crime. See, it was the case of the officer and a prostitute. Before our own eyes, we bore witness to the prostitute serving the needs of the officer. So that now best explains the game of "now you see her, now you don't." But wait, wasn't that our school? Wasn't that our sanctuary for learning? Oh wait, perhaps the biggest educational lesson for us was happening before our very eyes. Besides, mom and dad always told us that there were three senses we should strive to have: Book sense, common sense and that good ol' street sense.

I grew up on what is referred to as the south side of Chicago, in the historically known Woodlawn community. I have just one sibling, my brother, who's just short of two years younger than me. My neighborhood as historically rich as it was, maintained social diseases that only seemed to spread and worsen for each generation. I like to say it this way; my life today is one of two worlds, the streets and the suites. Ironically, this reality was lived well before my educational degrees. See, I grew up in the middle of "streets" and suites. Just two blocks north of me was one of the world's most prominent universities and two blocks south of me was the historic 63rd street infested with drugs, violence and brutality. So, in essence I grew up in the middle of two very different worlds, which inevitably challenged my decision-making early on in life. Which way should I go and whom would I turn to for success and survival?

Education in looking back was essential in "getting out." Interesting how such neighborhoods were seen as prisons, hence the language chosen of "getting out." Incredibly, if nothing else was clear, the need for better lives proved to be a major discussion on local blocks. As I have often taught in university settings, despite the rhetoric on Black people "acting White" when they received education, many people within our communities valued education. In the minds of many, education was that golden ticket out and when one was successful in school for instance, many applauded our efforts and wished all the more for our success. I look back and wonder how their "value" on education measured up to their own faith and ability to receive that same progress for their own lives. Some, I admit felt this golden ticket was not as valuable as was the gold jewelry around their necks or their wrist? Many others though, feared success because of the familiarity of failure all around them. Success had itself become an attainable goal for only a select few.

From where I sit, worthy of more analysis is this mindset that would on one hand advocate education as valuable, while simultaneously opting to not have it for one's self. Perhaps part of the answer is connected to the law-breaking police officer, his accomplice and their violation on our, oh so sacred school grounds. How could children in such environments take seriously their education in the face of such violations? The lack of respect shown to our school that day by the un-abiding law officer reflects an attitude that debatably gives birth to attitudes amongst our youth. Seemingly consistent that day from that police officer was a mentality of disregard for his law and my education. As he disrespected this law, he also violated my innocence and regard for education. Apparently, he served me this unfortunate memory and reality while again protecting his own interests.

Seemingly, I believe too many Americans live in poverty. Moreover, far too many Black Americans live in poverty and die because of poverty. In fact, it is my belief that poverty serves as a core issue to the many problems in our communities. For instance, poverty cannot afford that much needed, great attorney for the innocent child wrongfully arrested and charged. Poverty cannot seem to furnish necessary funds to pay for better schools for families desiring better education. Poverty is largely connected to how people eat and what they eat. Local grocery stores in these communities often sell older meats, bread and cheaper products void of any nutritional value. Is it then not surprising why so many of us live with high blood pressure, diabetes and obesity?

To those individuals demanding better choices from those living in poverty, I ask what are their chances in making greater choices? Poverty is evil and often prevents progress in its fullness. In fact, poverty leaves little room for healthy options to choose from. Here is more of my point: if my options for where I will live are nestled between two inner city housing developments on opposite ends of the town, then my decision is to choose one but they are both public housing developments. Even if my goals are to someday abandon such options, my reality is what I have before me now as options. So then my choices, even with the best decisions are limited. Thus, the impact of my success overall for my family is now connected to what that community has to offer me via its schools and other institutions. Simply stated, yes choices are important and even good decision making skills. Yet, what happens when your decisions are connected to limited options and choices? The following graph depicts my point:

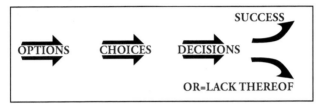

Our overall success, or lack thereof, in life is oftentimes intricately connected to things outside of us and around us. Living in and around poverty most often, and most detrimentally, produces an impoverished mindset. This mind of poverty helps produce the chains of bondage discussed in this book. Further, it is this mindset that must be challenged if any growth is to occur within such conditions and communities.

Consistent with how poverty impacts us, there must be some understanding on what any human being will resort to when unable to satisfy basic necessities in life. The stress of this alone provokes sleepless nights and serves as a thief to unlived dreams. I do not feel there is another generation within our cultural existence that has had to grapple with such terrorism, socially. Not many ethnic groups in America can relate to what it is like living in fear, afraid to send their children to neighborhood parks to play because of stray bullets. In fact, no other ethnic group has suffered in this country, for so long, so terribly. More specifically, the true travesty is found in being Black in a country that dehumanizes your skin color and race, being poor amongst oceans of wealth all around you and then growing up in what has been classified as "the 'hood" because of its shortage of neighbors making it a neighbor-hood, respectfully.

Obviously no true assessment can accurately depict our condition void of holding our people responsible for their own actions. This is far from my personal philosophy and my goal in writing this book. In several chapters I cover poverty as a basis of the chains and bondage. Specifically in the essay, Purchased Poverty, I address the thinking of a man in poverty verse a mind in poverty. In the end I boldly believe we have bought into our own poverty. An example of this is seen in our youth and their choices of material goods over magnificent grades. This is an individual piece we must critically challenge for our growth as a community. Yet we must continue to comprehend both sides of this argument on just how poverty works in our communities.

All the more, it is my philosophy to critically account for more than what we hear and see everyday, so my position is this; individuals are no more responsible for their condition than institutions are accountable for creating the condition. It is said best this way: Sure, individual girls (and her parents) seven years of age wearing halter tops and short shorts with "booty" on them need a conversation on modesty and the science of clothing. Too, however institutions should be held accountable in making such clothing available for seven-year old girls to wear. The real issue is found in companies that will produce such items for such ages.

Obviously, the issues before us are enormous. Please note that this is not just a "Black community" problem. This "laundry" when dirty, stains the nation. In fact, as we will explore here in this book, many of our issues are directly connected to America's issues. These challenges are rooted in a nation refusing to respect any others deemed non-White and many more that are not wealthy. Therein is the cause of this cancerous disease eating at the hearts and minds of many people in this country and most relevant to this book, Black people.

Champions Break Chains is written for those being asked to dream while living a nightmare. It is written for those seeking motivation in their lives because of the chains on their lives. What are the chains? The chains are the many things keeping us bound. Who are the champions? The champions are those with ultimate understanding of their chains, then choosing to live without excuse. One thing I know to be important is the necessity of change, which is significant to the heart of this book and even to the soul of our communities! As the champion in each of us seeks to blossom, we must challenge ourselves to be greater, to be stronger, to be wiser, to be better, then the change shall come to light. As we individually change ourselves, so shall our families and communities change. Again, this is not a Black issue alone. As we save and heal Black folk in this country today, so shall we save and heal America's tomorrow. Truly, "we are only as strong as our weakest link." We must break these chains of bondage for the sake of establishing stronger links in the chain that connects us all. In the end, no one will save us but us.

BLACKADEMICALLY
SPEAKING

Blackademically Speaking is about voice—my voice and thoughts on the pulse of the Black community. Admittedly, I fall short of speaking as a scholarly academic, in that I attempt to "make the complex very simple". My goal isn't to arm the reader with theories or rigorous rubric. This language is precariously foreign to the millions of Americans that are illiterate and hopeless. Blackademically Speaking seeks to tenderly address the hearts and minds of those, while speaking *"their language."*

Champions Break Chains draws from the urban vernacular, unapologetically. I write for those in urban communities who are interested in thinking outside the box to challenge and change their conditions. My targeted audience are those in jails and under-performing schools. I also target the smart child who knows little about their history. I dare to reach those individuals who may not like to read. My audience is widespread. He/she must be willing to accept a different way to communicate today's issues. Being that my voice as a motivational speaker is non-academic and non-traditional, I carry the same torch here as an author.

I welcome the academician, my colleagues to speak Blackademically. I invite you to shift your focus in reading this book, as it is not written for publication in refereed journals. My goal is to capture the attention of urban youth nationwide. Truth is, many of the articles and books written by scholars, lack an authentic capacity to solve the issues our children are coping with daily.

Blackademically Speaking helps translate important academic work for liberation into a language of importance for those needing liberation. In other words, Blackademically Speaking is somewhat of a bridge; it is a charismatic concept in dealing with a cultural crisis. To put it short, our children are dying! So, it is an audacious task to strike a balance between my two worlds, leaning heavily to my love for urban communities.

Blackademically Speaking is concerned about the future of Black folk in this country and humanity in general. Blackademically Speaking is a theoretical response to scholars who insist on trying to own what is rigorous and acceptable. I obviously respect academia and higher education. Nevertheless, I value the Black backs I stand on that fought and died for me to achieve the right to speak in this capacity—those same backs that made it possible for me to attain the level of education I have to date.

It is the voice of my ancestry that carries me to this platform. It is their ideas and philosophy that Blackademically Speaking yields to. It is the voice of enslaved Harriet Tubman crying from the plantation, demanding freedom for not only herself but too, the many she refused to leave behind. It is the voice of Attorney Sadie T.M. Alexander… Dorothy Height…Mary McLeod Bethune shouting, "**knowledge is the prime need of the hour**" and "**the drums of Africa still beat in my heart. They will not let me rest while there is a single Negro boy or girl without a chance to prove his worth.**" It is the voice of activist and journalist Ida B. Wells who seventy-one years before Rosa Parks refused to give up her seat and soon being dragged by two men from the train car, she would later pen the following regarding her writings and work for the people:

> I had an instinctive feeling that the people who have little
> or no school training should have something coming into
> their homes weekly which dealt with their problems in a
> simple, helpful way...so I wrote in a plain, common-sense
> way on the things that concerned our people.

It is this synergy Blackademically Speaking builds on and connects to. It is this ancestry that I acknowledge, affirm and aim to speak with. It is their voices, silenced as women yet soaring on as change agents, determined and dedicated to deal with the issues of the time.

Few white scholars dare to understand the levels of rejection experienced by Black folk throughout the centuries of our existence here in America. Even fewer white scholars care to honestly account for the factors that have imprisoned our people in chains of bondage. Blackademically Speaking refuses to travel on this highway of scholarship. No, Black folk have not arrived! Blackademically Speaking is thus my dutiful contribution to a serious work for freedom that has never been unnecessary, despite the gains we have made. My generation is nothing more than beneficiaries of assassinated leadership, who risked their lives for our current and limited successes. Our generation in appearing most successful professionally looks through the window of failure, socially and communally. We must decide how we will challenge the constant demon of racism and the perpetual diseases associated with it.

Blackademically Speaking is one such decision. It makes no excuses for America and how it continues to portray and treat Black people, nor does it make any excuses for Black folk and how we treat one another. Blackademically Speaking is best read as thought-provoking pieces of work. The various essays written in each of these twelve chapters are in strong critique of Black culture, yet motivational; thus to speak Blackademically is to speak critically and honestly with doses of courage for our culture and hope for our hearts.

Champions Break Chains highlights many issues within Black, inner city communities and families. Blackademically Speaking is the tool and voice used to describe these issues while daring you to re-think what has been common and comfortable. For instance, it is my belief that proper education is in fact essential to our survival. However I submit to you that too many of our schools fail in the area of educating our children due to imbalanced emphasis on curriculum goals. Today's inner city child demands social, psychological and personal attention. Contrary to foolish philosophy, this attention is not due to the child being "special" or dumb; the attention here is important because of the circumstances our children are immersed in daily that hurt their educational experience. It is very difficult to focus on getting a 'B' in subject matter when you can't just B(e) a child. Many of our children live in hostile homes and very hectic communities. Their norms growing up are at best abnormal, yet common.

Blackademically Speaking supports educating the whole child for liberation, while providing them necessary motivation. Again, it is difficult to learn physics when the *gravity* of your life is imbalanced and impoverished—it is an even greater challenge to learn mathematical concepts when the violence and abuse around you *multiplies* your pain and *divides* you from your purpose; in the end, it just doesn't *add* up. Bottom line, our children need motivation beyond their situation. Coupled with proper education, our children will soar.

Above all, Blackademically Speaking is the spiritual headliner representing these tenets of motivation. So in reading this book, be prepared for culturally relevant education on various issues, coupled with motivation for your mind and spirit beyond the issues. We all need an extra push, an encouraging word and an understanding heart. Life's curve balls can create despair; however, we must note that our misery is most often connected to our ministry. No matter how many degrees I sought to attain, Blackademically Speaking was sadly, yet beautifully born out of the following reality:

Ph.D. Felon

With 6.6 seconds left and the game now tied with a 3 pointer scored for our team, a time out is called. A cold January night now comes down to this. Can we pull off the victory, in this growing rivalry? Wait, who is this guy talking to my friend? What does he want with her? Towered over my co-advisor of our teen group is a tall man speaking through the cheers and loudness of others in the gym. With aim to hear the conversation between the two in these ascending bleachers, I leaned over. Soon thereafter, handcuffs were flashed from whom we later learn to be an off-duty cop at this high school basketball game. Enter next, an on-duty female officer to arrest my co-advisor. As they escort her out of the gym, I calm my mentees, the teenagers of our youth group and also students of this very high school we found ourselves mentoring in this Friday night. I recall only saying, "Lord help me."

After grabbing my belongings to leave the gym, I was met at the door by the same guy initiating this interesting exchange. He demanded that I go back into the gym. I calmly suggested to him that I was preparing to leave considering the game nearing its end. As to not belabor the point here, I hone in on that very guy, later learned to be an off-duty cop, choking me into a seizure I had that night.

At the tender age of 12 years old after my brother's birthday party, I passed out. The reason at the time was speculative. Three months later the same blackout occurred, this time leading to various doctor's appointments, tests and examinations for the cause. An incidental finding was discovered. Still unsure as to the reason for what was deemed seizure activity, a tumor was found on my pituitary gland. Several months and even years later, specialists and other physicians immersed themselves in researching these two health issues. I was diagnosed with having two separate issues and prescribed Phenobarbital to control my epileptic activity. My involvement in sports and other physical activity was soon limited and I was cautioned against stress related things, situations and events.

Perhaps had the off-duty cop known this history, he would have taken heed to those adages of my inner city community by "keeping his hands to himself." What had I done to ignite such behavior from this officer? That Friday night, when many of my peers were embarking upon their weekend socially, there I sat as a volunteer for high school students. For years I had served as advisor of this youth group while in undergraduate and now graduate school, downstate Illinois. I was blessed to develop beautiful and lasting relationships with parents of these young women who simply sought opportunity and positive exposure for their daughters. I was adjoined to a sorority dedicated to leaving the world much better than how they found it. This very organization for youth was at the core of what we believe. It was what I participated in at that tender age and now I had the opportunity to "give back." Community service was important as I diligently sought to help others in the surrounding community. In fact, before my membership in the sorority, I worked side-by-side with some of its members, as it was known that I participated in this youth group as a high school student in Chicago. The campus-aged women of the sorority sought to bring this national initiative for young ladies to the local community. My dedication that Friday night was thus common and consistent to what I had been involved with for some time.

Perhaps it would not have mattered if that cop knew any of this. Did it matter that I was at the time President of two organizations and Advisor for three others on campus and in the community, ranging from ministry to student associations? Was it relevant that I was no criminal? Did it matter that I was only leaving the game while checking on my co-advisor and friend, too a graduate student and my sorority sister? Clearly my anti-criminal behavior and background was significant and relevant. My parents responsibly taught me the importance of "right and wrong" and they insisted that I always walk upright.

As I lay there on the floor as a substitute teacher for this very high school, I recall hearing voices. Moments later, I felt this outside breeze. I was coming out of my seizure. Tears fell from my eyes, as they do now in writing this. Somehow healing as a process takes time beyond time. I murmured my name to these strangers when asked. I realized I was being wheeled to the ambulance. While there, I am told to "stop faking." Afraid and nervous, I began to shake my head. Strong emotions pulled me into remembrance of this seizure activity I had so long avoided. It had been fifteen years since my last seizure, yet it was all so familiar. I continued to shake my head with tears rolling down my face in response to this unusually strict paramedic. "Boss," I hear. I am oddly alone riding in the ambulance. Where are my parents? Where is a familiar face? The paramedic to my left insists that I am faking as he checks my vitals. I continue to shake my head as if to say, "no." I am unable to speak clearly yet my attempt is strong. He cuts the sleeve of my shirt enforcing his belief of me faking. My mouth is pried open by another with a tool being shoved down my throat. What was this? Why was this happening? What had I done? "If you think this was bad, wait till you get in here" were the words left for me to ponder in being wheeled from the ambulance.

My life was changed that cold January night. Here I now lay, hospitalized after being choked by a cop and further victimized by medical officials. Were they not as professionals responsible for helping me to feel better? What was their motivation in stepping outside of their professional duty as caretakers, having me feel isolated and afraid? After being escorted into the hospital room, I recall seeing police officers, nurses and doctors. Still without a familiar face, I was fearful. Sadly, I was treated as some animal that night. I recall asking a nurse for help. As I lay there, I witnessed conversations amongst these people. What were they expressing to one another?

As I communicated to a nurse my name, date of birth and other relevant information, I with all the energy I could muster, asked to call my mom. I was denied any outside contact for what seemed like hours. Sadly, what came of it all per my treatment was a urine sample request. In the many years as a patient in this very hospital, it seems as if someone would pull my medical records. Yet, the only test taken regarding my condition that night was for alcohol or drug levels. Not one tests or examination was given specific to my seizure history. I was emotionally drained and physically tortured.

"You are under arrest." These words remain etched in my memory still today. With my pastor and his wife at my bedside, the police officer demanded my arrest on a charge of mob action. I was astounded and petrified all at the same time. My pastor insisted things would be fine. He ensured that I would be released by daybreak.

This remains for me the night of unfamiliar; Unfamiliar faces plus unfamiliar treatment resulted in unfamiliar circumstances. Ironically and sadly each of these public officials responsible for carrying out respectable duties violated their professional roles that cold night. I was now met with an unfamiliar territory, the jail cell. It was here where I was reconnected with my co-advisor who explained to me the behavior of the officer that night at the school. I had vague memories as I obviously blacked out as a result of the seizure. So there we sat, Ph.D. students of the flagship university of the state, now in jail. I guess this was our bogus reward for working hard as student-volunteers within our college community. Moreover, because of what I had learned in my college classrooms sociologically, this behavior and attitude was recognizable.

What happens when that of what you learn in classrooms and witness in your immediate environment becomes your reality? How was I able to escape the many problems of my inner-city community at home where there existed greater chances of failure, only to arrive on a college campus and endure the very things I thought I left behind? Jail had become the end result for so many back home, yet never my reality. Now I was somehow in the same predicament as a Ph.D. student striving for success.

My pastor and so many others that next morning awaited my hearing for bond. I stood before a teleprompter as the judge read new charges of Aggravated Battery and Obstructing a Peace Officer. The irony was centered on these new and elevated charges coupled with a bond of recognizance. Said a different and more poignant way, I was now charged with more serious charges, yet released on an I-bond. My major charge, a Class 3 felony, was specific to the off-duty cop implying I choked him the night before.

With several court appearances that next week, I immediately hired attorneys. I was indicted on my birthday just days after my release from jail. My life had become oddly similar to the very lives I encouraged others not to live. I had lived a life of servitude. I, as an avid volunteer of the community offered much more than tuition. I took seriously what my parents had instilled in me; I was dedicated to helping others strive beyond their circumstances.

My life so dedicated to the youth of that community was now centered on my own freedom. Monthly court appearances and meetings with attorneys became a major addition to my studies. I was slated to complete my Master's degree that very semester. This was obviously halted. "Consider a plea bargain," was what my attorney echoed along with so many respectable community leaders. "Don't fight the system, you will never win," rang from the mouths of "Believers" representing my faith. Why would I admit to something I had not done? What would come of such admission? Why would I bow down? These and so many other questions plagued my mind. I knew I had to stand for what I believed in. I knew the strength of my attitude focused on principle was important. Moreover, my reputation of courage and faith preceded me. What message would it send the youth I had long taught and mentored? Why would I succumb to pressures, despite their alleged power and admit to what had not truly taken place? Did I not believe in truth and honesty? Was I not courageous enough with my own life to live out principles beyond the sermons and lectures I gave for their lives as young citizens? I declared to fight.

My challenges were real. The thought of a conviction plagued me often. Yet this was not my focus. My eyes were on my principles and not my pain. I was depressed. I sought counseling on campus. I cried. I was angry. I questioned God. Yet, I walked in courtroom hearings with my head held high, bible in hand believing in my quest for justice irrespective of the 3-5 year sentence before me. Continuance after continuance, I left the courtroom hearings afraid, yet affirmed. My support was grand. Dozens would show up with me in the name of justice. My attorney would later withdraw from the case. She personally insisted that she admired my faith yet could not stand the chance of a possible conviction. "I wouldn't be able to live with myself," were her words spoken. The challenges seemed greater by the day. The thought of losing my chances to graduate college because of a felony conviction made things all the more frightening. With little knowledge of my future as a Ph.D. student, I still refused any plea-bargaining. My conviction was Spirit-led despite any conviction the court would render unto me.

My co-advisor had become my co-defendant. We agreed that we would fight the battle. We clashed often ideologically and personally with our attorney. Her decision to later withdraw as our attorney confirmed our doubts. We also learned of a personal relationship between one of the partners at the firm, another attorney, and the very cop responsible for choking me. She did not see the conflict and even questioned our trust with her. We questioned confidentiality and an obvious conflict of interest. She soon fired us and we pressed on.

Nineteen months after that cold, January night we were set for trial. We opted for a jury trial. A jury of our peers seemed obsolete. Our selection pool was minus an opportunity to select one with perhaps cultural clarity. There was not one Black in the pool. A non-Black jury pool for Black defendants was the message sent at the onset of this trial. The selection began. The trial lasted four days. Many people took the stand. Character witnesses from the university, unfamiliar faces that witnessed the behavior of the cops that night and our teenaged mentees took the stand on our behalf. Included in the number were two state troopers compelled to testify to the behavior of their fellow officers. Attesting to having not witnessed such an abuse of power in their near 50 years of service collectively, the message was going forward regarding our innocence that night.

Not to be outdone, the first witness for the state was a Black face and school official insisting things totally out of context to that night. As a fan at the game, he insisted that my co-defendant resisted arrest, one of her two charges. His position on the stand as their first witness sent yet another racialized message to us. Nonetheless, the highlight for us was when the officer in question was unable to identify us in the courtroom. He insisted that my co-defendant was the one who choked him that night. If the officer cannot identify his assailant, is there not a question to what he alleges happened? Further, how grounded were these charges considering his obscure memory of something so critical to his livelihood, security and health? Our request of tossing the case was denied. After much testimony, my co-advisor was convicted on her misdemeanor charge of Resisting Arrest and reprieved of her felony charge. I was convicted on the felony charge of Aggravated Battery and reprieved of my misdemeanor:

> "We, the jury, find defendant, Chandra Gill, not guilty
> of Obstructing a Peace Officer." "We, the jury, find the
> defendant, Chandra Gill, guilty of Aggravated Battery."

Sentencing was set for two months to the date.

In reading like some nightmare, this story is no story. For so many people the judicial system is a nightmare. In my opinion, the issue of incarceration is the human rights issue of our time. As explored here in my first section, abolishing slavery institutionally led to what I deem mental incarceration individually. The chains left the ankles for the mind. Those chains encourage fear, doubt and cowardice. Those very chains aim to battle the act of winning and faith. Champions enjoy winning, thus losing is emotionally, professionally and even spiritually challenging. Champions find it hard to quit. Champions learn the art of winning and work hard to do so. I had to thus champion my quest for freedom against a disastrous system seeking to steal my faith and will to win in life.

Today, the battle for so many is similar in that it is a fight to live faithfully and think freely. Champions understand this and refuse to allow the mind to be arrested, charged, sentenced and convicted. What the city convicted and later sentenced was my body; I insisted that my mind belonged to me.

Although desiring to make of me an example, as stated by the prosecution the day of my sentencing, I was sentenced to 18 months conditional discharge. Armed with nearly 200 character letters, I sent the message to the court and the judge that I was no criminal. I was not a felon as I had learned in counseling and I was a champion. That of what I had known to champion my entire life was centered on being fair, loving and just. Many friends, family members, co-workers and colleagues attested to my character. My sentencing, albeit frightening, could not deter me from my goal of achieving my degrees.

Many reading this will say I received support that so many others do not have. Others have argued that my status as a student rendered privileges unto me not granted for so many deserving others. I acknowledge the power of my support system as they encouraged me throughout. This support helped bring out the best in me. I now insist that what we go through and label as misery, is the very place we should accept as our ministry. Could it be that what we experience despite the unjustness of it all can actually be used for the just fight in it all? My battle itself proved unnecessary in that no one should fall victim to such evil. Yet it was necessary in that my perspective shifted to best appreciate the test of my faith as God carried me through.

From where I sit, sports encourage what classrooms and communities should use as example; Winning is the best option and we should never accept failure no matter how tough the opponent seems. With sports as my parallel and fittingly since I too played team sports, I leave you with this; the starting five of a basketball team are typically the best at their positions. When a team wins a championship, the starting five does not earn a ring greater and shinier than those on the bench. Champions on the team, with the team encourage what is necessary for the team to win the championship. True champions encourage winning, period. If you should happen to be on the team with the best player in the nation, you are identified with a champion. If you never play one minute the entire year, you are still a teammate. In fact it is imperative that you practice and prepare in case of accident or damage to a fellow teammate. While you are not the better player, you await your opportunity. If this time never presents itself, and the team wins the championship, you will still enter history as a part of the championship team.

Many may tell you to quit, since the coach will not give you playing time. Others may suggest that you hang in there until the appointed time. One of the greatest athletes to ever play the game of basketball, Michael Jordan, was once cut from his high school team. He arose to greatness because of a championship spirit and later became a championship player. Had he accepted the coach's evaluation of him, we would not speak of him and his glorious greatness on the court. So in that, guess what? His cut was necessary. Yes, I said it; the cut was necessary. Being cut from the team, I surmise challenged the champion in him.

Many could say that it was only possible because he was destined for greatness. Others could argue differently. As with my situation, we learn that the elements around us are simply not stronger than what is within us. In fact, were it not for the test of those elements against us, would we ever know just how great we really are? The hearts of champions continually seek victory in war despite any loss in battle. My faith proved strong and increased over time. In hindsight I now believe I was momentarily benched by the system; my friends and family coached me as I achieved the ring which was my mental and physical freedom. So, for me the felony was *necessary*...

"I freed a thousand slaves. I could have freed a thousand more if only they had known they were slaves."

—**Harriet Tubman**

? - ?

Imagine not knowing the day you were born. Further, imagine your life being as irrelevant as your death. Slavery as America's greatest evil denied Africans their God-given right in being treated as human beings. Although many in our country today like to dismiss slavery as old news, we begin with these two question marks and the hyphen that separates them.

The two question marks represent a date of birth and a date of death. Does it make any sense to you? Okay so how about the hyphen that I insist symbolizes all of the anguish and pain lived in a place never welcoming you nor treating you with dignity and respect. What does it really feel like having your family's history rooted in the unknown and the unworthy? One of my more popular lectures is, "Whats in a Name." It is in this lecture that I challenge my students to build their family tree. In starting with their name at the top of the page I ask that they list their mom and dad's full name thereafter. From there I ask that they list their mom's mom and dad on one side, while on the other side listing their dad's mom and dad. As this is done I, of course, challenge them in continuing on as far as they can while also listing birthdays of each of these persons named.

Sadly, many of my students have found themselves unable to list their own father's name, let alone their grandparents or great-grand parents. Keep in mind, I teach non-traditional students who are not all fresh from high school classrooms. My students range in age from 21 to 70 *years*.

This is a critical point in that I have learned that slavery cannot stand as just this thing of the past when still far too many of us feel its effects. Without an ability to name and place your own parents and grandparents, life can be rather devastating. This devastation is something we have learned to live with. Yet it is remarkably painful when we spend just a little time discussing the horrors of slavery and why we are disconnected from our own family.

It is neither fair nor feasible to buy into the hype of slavery being an irrelevant discussion today when it is at the root of many issues. Here it is important to note that slaves were auctioned off and sold as property. Often those enslaved were sold away from their own family members. Fathers were taken away from families while mothers were stripped of their children. Women were marketed and placed on plantations to pick cotton in fields by day while also helping raise the master's children. Adding insult to this, these same women were often raped by their slave master and forced to have his children. Despite the slave master being the biological father of such children, these babies would enter the world as slaves void of human rights. As I see it, this sounds a lot like the 'baby daddy' discussions of today.

In the fabric of slavery's evil is a reality of how names were then taken and changed to the master's liking while birthdays were not acknowledged. Try telling any child in America today that they do not have a birthday. Now consider yourself having little knowledge of your birth date. Slavery is the ultimate thief of Black folk's lineage and contributions to this country. For me, that first question mark represents the plantation and the last one represents the cemetery. Both of these land filled spaces ironically over the years refused dignity to those of African decent. Ask yourself, why cemeteries in America would refuse Black folk an opportunity to be buried respectfully? Oddly, Blacks were heartlessly treated after death the same as they were while alive.

With the plantation as our beginning and the cemetery as our end we must best understand the whopping effects of how we have been forced to live our lives here in America. In being denied our proper birthrights and declined from burial grounds simply based on the color of our skin, it is the hyphen that is important. History reminds us of the importance inliving in fullness; for it is in how we live, that tells the ultimate story. It is true that the hyphen for our people has been one of pain, sorrow and sadness. It is the hyphen that speaks to the likes and works of so many who died fighting for justice. It is the hyphen in Medgar Evers who courageously fought side by side with White soldiers in Europe for America and its war, only to return to America's soil to be murdered in front of his own home at the tender age of 37. Fighting for civil rights in his own country proved more dangerous than fighting an actual war on foreign land. It is the hyphen in 14-year-old Chicagoan Emmett Till who, after a visit to his family in the South, returned home an unrecognizable corpse because he supposedly whistled at a White woman. Having one eye gouged out, his head crushed and a bullet lodged in it, it is the hyphen experience of his mother Mamie Till that speaks today. Her courage, convicts us as she spoke about her son's murder, "Have you ever sent a loved son on vacation and had him returned to you in a pine box, so horribly battered and water-logged that someone needs to tell you this sickening sight is your son — lynched?"

Yes, it is the hyphen that we must acknowledge, appreciate and become more acquainted with. We cannot afford to ignore the short lived and saddened hyphened experiences of so many who solely desired respect. The hyphen begs the question of a country like America that must ultimately be questioned. It is thus the hyphen in America's livelihood as a nation that we critique. It is the first question mark of America's life that I feel represents its birth as a racist nation. In enslaving human beings, that first question mark has led to the tragic hyphen experiences of so many Blacks in this country. It is the hyphen experience of us as a people today that must challenge and change this country's current hyphen or live out its unquestionable fate of its second question mark—a date we know to be destined for judgment by God.

"COTTON PICKING" IS NO CONCEPT

Repeat after me, slavery was an institution! Got it? Okay, let's do it again (say it slowly), *slavery was an institution.* What's important about this fact? What does this mean? By definition, institutions are united for specified purposes, oftentimes for the promotion of some cause. This institution of slavery once occurring on America's soil was evil and responsible for the death of many, many Africans. As with many institutions it bore a function. Its function was the promotion of inferiority amongst those enslaved for the sake of production. Cotton was the product and those enslaved were the responsible parties for such production all day, every day and free of charge.

Instilling fear in the heart of those enslaved was extremely important to the maintenance of slavery as an institution. Africans were whipped, beaten, and murdered for unbelievable and inhumane reasons. Many risked losing their lives for the sake of learning to read, write or even attempting to escape.

Harriet Tubman, albeit known for her tenacity in freeing slaves, is one of such examples. She is one whom many know of and not enough about. Ask yourself, if you lived in slavery would you have really had the heart to risk your life for freedom? Think long and hard about the question! Now ask yourself, if your answer is yes, whether after reaching the North you would have mustered the courage to take a trip back only to aid others in getting to their land of freedom as well? Would you continue a second time? How about a third? How many trips would you have taken? More than a hundred years later, it is quite intriguing to sit and consider what we would have possibly done had that been us. Many of us are quick to say what we would have not tolerated had we been enslaved:

> **Person 1:** "Man, please, there's no way I would have let nobody put their hands on me like that!"
>
> **Person 2:** "Sounds good—you would have done just what everybody else had to do."
>
> **Person 1:** "NO I wouldn't...I ain't nobody's punk."
>
> **Person 2:** "Yeah, it's easy to say that now."

Such exchanges are common amongst Black folk in discussions on slavery and their roles if they themselves were enslaved. Much is even said about those that escaped or fought back, the likes of Nat Turner and Frederick Douglass. The truth is despite, the courageous stance we feel that we could and should have taken; the chains of slavery were very strong. Africans arriving on foreign soil were thrust into one of the most evil acts committed against mankind. Sister Harriet like so many other daring souls chose to break those chains for her ultimate freedom and with others in mind. In suggesting that she would have freed many more slaves, our beloved and courageous sister acknowledges something very important—THE MIND! She references eloquently the mindset of those choosing to remain enslaved. Here I assert one great reason for their decision to stay back—fear!

HARRIET TUBMAN WAS FREE
BEFORE SHE WAS FREE

Too easily, many today suggest that they would have accompanied Sister Harriet out of and away from life in chains; it is easy to believe such in hindsight. This is believable due to the imagery we have been presented about slavery. Specific to my point, many have faith in what would have been their escape then because they imagine solely breaking chains from their body while meeting up with Harriet in the forest. Their thoughts coincide with following the trail of the Underground Railroad led by the North Star. The truth many fail to understand is that freedom for many of those enslaved existed in the mind first. The mind was forced to conquer the very fear used as a tool to keep them in bondage. This was no small task. Furthermore, few willingly parallel the power of those chains to today's struggle for many. Again, this is due to how many of us misinterpret slavery and all of its effects. Few of us know much about the day-to-day operation of this institution and its very tactics. Harriet, however, realized that she was enslaved. Most significant here is her mental freedom that preceded her bodily freedom. I submit to you, my readers that her body could not go where her mind was not ready to guide her. She first had to declare she was enslaved, and then came the challenge of conquering the fear of escape. Lastly, she had to make up in her mind COMPLETELY that she not only deserved freedom, but was willing to die getting it. So we learn immediately that even when your body is in chains, the brain must first break the bondage! People, I am going somewhere with my point here; Harriet was free before she was free!

She declared in her mind FIRST that the very institution enslaving her would not keep her for long. The institution was accountable only to the laws best benefiting the slave master. The slaves "had no rights that the white man was bound to respect." This statement made in 1857 by Chief Justice Roger B. Taney of the United States Supreme Court best depicts the nation's posture regarding slaves. The Dred Scott case featuring this infamous position of a Supreme Court judge draws attention to the very thinking of America's "powers that be" at the time! Yet, Harriet Tubman, first in her mind, despite the law supporting the institution, declared that freedom was her goal. Not only so, it became her reality and the precursor to her physical freedom. Simply put, Sister Harriet Tubman sought not to spend her life:

—◇◇—

1] dwelling on the problems of slavery.

2] wondering when and if somebody would come and free her from slavery.

3] thinking that the laws would soon, someday, somehow change because some one...somewhere else...cared about her enslavement.

—◇◇—

She believed in her GOD-given right to be free and freed her mind first.

CHAINS ON THE BRAIN

During slavery, clearly the majority of slaves knew they were slaves, at least physically. How could they not? They witnessed their kind being attacked by vicious slaveholders day in and day out. Being forced to work for free only to earn scraps called meals. Taking lashes for the silliest of things and entering slave auctions only to be bought and sold away from their family. These evil acts surely intensified the horror of this institution.

Although physically enslaved, few of our ancestors comprehended the totality, the breadth of mental enslavement and its long-lasting effects. Arguably, even fewer were willing to risk their lives for freedom. Now let's state here that choosing to stay back was not altogether cowardice. In fact, considering the major consequences of being caught, the slave had much to consider. More to the point, however, are the interesting threats before the slave. Fear, as stated, was invoked daily as slaves watched fellow slaves, even family members, beaten publicly as reminders of what could and would happen to them. Another major dynamic of slavery that kept the institution real and relevant was the ignorance of the slave. If caught teaching and or learning how to read and write, slaves risked death. This was largely enforced and speaks volume to my point.

One of the major victories for the institution of slavery was its ability to keep slaves illiterate through the lens of fear. Fear + Illiteracy almost always equaled constant enslavement. When we look at today's predicament for urban youth, it is rather intriguing and necessary to parallel the chains of slavery then to the chains on many now.

I recall being asked, "Dr. Gill do you really think slavery has anything to do with these kids and the way that they act today?" My response I share with you here: "Absolutely." As I engaged in discussion supporting my response, I recall thinking and even concluding with that particular individual this way, "Truly, we better 'blame' this behavior on something." What I was suggesting was neither blamelessness nor denial. The position was simple. From hanging on street corners for the same amount of time you can be in school, to spending money on rims for wheels costing more than the price of the car itself, such behavior has to be rooted in something. For me, such mentality is easily adjoined and even chained to systems that provoke thinking of inferiority. This is not solely the case, as we will discuss in chapter two. Pertinent though is further investigation on how overwhelmingly God's children wind up in jails and not colleges, on corners and not in classrooms and pregnant with babies at 13, yet not pregnant with hope, faith and opportunity.

A large challenge for many people today is recognizing the chains as chains. Chains adjoin. Chains connect. Chains have the awesome power and ability to lock down and lock up. Chains in this context maintain levels of enslavement associated with bondage. Chains on one's brain perpetuates ignorance. This can lead to academic and educational underachievement.

It also places strong limitations on a child's otherwise promising future. Chains on the brain is a metaphoric powerhouse, insisting that our right to freely think is suppressed by outside forces. Think about the foolishness we witness in our communities and ultimately in our country. One thing is certain, America's citizens are all subjected to this bondage; thus there are many needing to break the chains. There are more who must learn how to live as champions. Talk show hosts make millions helping folk navigate through their problems. More times than none, these problems are rooted in breaking the chains of failure, overeating, debt, choosing the wrong mate over and over again, low expectations, suicide, death, loneliness, ugliness, racism, sexism, drugs, abuse, etc.

I submit that much of who we are and what we do is connected to how we were raised and what we were raised around. Your past will only determine your future if you consciously refuse to change your present. If in your household you were never taught very important life skills, your ability to thus manage in life is challenged. Better, if you are not taught how to critically think, then your daily decisions are unquestioned, leading to social patterns and behavior that mimic the exact opposite of your inherent genius. In going back to the culture of standing on corners sunup to sundown, for many it is the corner in urban context where much of the action occurs. Seldom are our youth considering the time wasted in trivial conversations on 'the block' with risks of being arrested, in contrast to making better use of that same time being productive academically. I ask this question of my kings standing on corners: if you can exert so much energy and time on a corner you do not own while living outside the will of God, can you imagine what awaits you if you begin to exert that same energy toward what you were actually created to do within the will of God?

This issue and behavior is not solely attributed to your being nonchalant about life or indifferent; the problem is rooted in an unchanged mind coupled with unchanged schools and unchanged parents. It is connected to a failed curriculum that refuses to address your ultimate value specific to your royal heritage. Consequently, your environment produces failure and hopelessness. This ultimately cripples your thinking. To shift this unfortunate truth, rid yourself of limiting goals such as holding down corners with a false sense of power. Remove the chains, brothers and sisters. As you gamble on these corners shooting dice and laughing, you are crapping out in life and the joke is on us as a people.

"BLACK" HISTORY
IS WORLD HISTORY

Have you ever wondered why Black History Month was chosen as the month to celebrate Blacks in history? Why the shortest month of the year? What is Black history anyway? Are we suggesting that Black folk have their own history? The acknowledgment of this month for Black folks was born out of a need to acknowledge the achievements of those of African blood. In 1926, it began as Negro History Week. Carter G. Woodson selected February and the week between Frederick Douglass and President Abraham Lincoln's birthdays. Fifty years later it became Black History Month. It is very interesting to note the extreme relevance of how Carter G. Woodson largely educated himself, taking seriously this aspect of his life. In one of his many works, he later suggested the following:

> "When you control a man's thinking you do not have to
> worry about his actions. You do not have to tell him not
> to stand here or go yonder. He will find his 'proper place'
> and will stay in it. You do not need to send him to the
> back door. He will go without being told. In fact, if there
> is no back door, he will cut one for his special benefit.
> His education makes it necessary."
>
> —*The Mis-Education of the Negro,* 1933

As the second Black in the history of Harvard University to receive his Ph.D. in History, Dr. Woodson proved to be a very powerful thinker. As you see in this quote, written nearly 80 years ago, we must think clearly; our freedom and liberation rests on our ability to think critically.

As witnessed throughout this book, we know the powerful effects our thinking has, specific to our conditions. The chains of slavery, once loosed from the slave's body, achieved little in penetrating the thinking of slave owners who would only see them as mere property. So, as Africans were released from this legal torture, they were essentially served to a sea of wolves, uneducated, yet empowered and determined. More to the point, the mindset of the slave owners and other Whites were as significantly detrimental to mankind as were the mindsets of enslaved Africans.

Africans and their contributions to the world predate slavery in America and the scope of this work. Most relevant is my point on how our genius sustained itself despite the suffering and enslavement of our culture. How beautiful is it to tell our children that even the plantation failed in robbing us of our resilience. Actually, the more i think about it, I feel America's evildoers should be thankful. Had their mission with slavery lasted, would they have the bonus of our intelligence on America's social issues. To my people i say this, we survived slavery, the most evil act against mankind. What more have we not seen as a result of our inherited brilliance and resilience? What kind of people actually survives such?

So what happened to such genius? How does one emerge from a lineage of erecting pyramids only to lie dormant at the knees of mediocrity? Clearly, the history of a people and the mis-education of the same promise little for minds that do not know who they are.

Further perpetuating this problem is a nation that knowingly mis-educates and misguides its citizens. As with slavery, such philosophy destroys not just those enslaved, but also those responsible for the enslavement. Many non-African people in the world deny the brilliance of African folk because of educated ignorance. Stereotypical views of Black folk reign in total opposition to their contributions to not only America, but to the world. I submit that if we are to conceal and bind the gifts of African people to the world, then we should eliminate the usage of their contributions as well. I give you this to affirm my point: Charles Drew gave the field of science necessary advancements relative to blood and plasma transfusions. His knowledge on the matter revolutionized the thinking of the time and thus aided in saving countless lives up to the present day. George Washington Carver, an agricultural researcher, is accredited for his many discoveries within the field of science. Familiar to some as the one deriving over three hundred products from the peanut, he actually gave the world well over five hundred products, with his study of the peanut, pecan and sweet potato.

If these African men are not worthy of inclusion in schools and curricula then certainly we should eliminate the usage of what they gave the world. I hear of no one desiring to utilize their contributions only for the month of February, so why only *celebrate their existence in that month?* Should we only consume Carver's products in February? These Black men were not simply amongst the greatest of Black people; they were amongst the greatest of all people! We can indeed commemorate their works in this spectacular month, yet we can celebrate their contributions and gifts throughout the year as well.

Few people, Black, White, Asian or Latino know much of Black folk beyond stereotypical imagery. This is tragic as this very imagery hijacks our lineage of greatness The chains of ignorance forcefully isolates Blacks from World History subject matter. Black history is not for Blacks only, just as Whites in history are not solely for Whites. Blacks and their contributions to the world are utilized by an entire world. If all people are blessed by their contributions, surely they should know from whom they are blessed. Eleven months cannot ignore what one month could never fairly and thoroughly inform.

- TWO -
〈〉〈〉

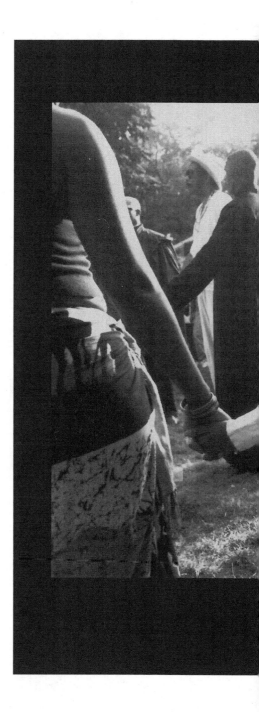

[Black Religion ⏐ Black Faith]

Photo courtesy of Jamel Shabazz

CHAINS OF PAIN

So, where is God in all of this madness? Why are we experiencing so much pain, so much sorrow? Ask anyone in our communities these questions and you are sure to get a multitude of answers. Truthfully, the conversation from my end deals with the generational pain we have experienced. My dad, as the oldest of sixteen children, would often speak of the pain he experienced while growing up in Chicago's housing projects on the south side. Battling heavy forces of gang activity, crime, and poverty, he often referenced the struggle for survival. His dad, my granddaddy, desired higher education. There was just one problem; high school for Blacks in a segregated south was not an option. Growing up in Arkansas provided few options for his overall success as a young Black man.

Their life experiences further enhanced their desires to see my brother and I achieve educationally. Granddaddy would frequently convey his love for education to me, mentioning his passionate desire to someday become a doctor. He said he always envisioned helping sick people and, of course, healing his family. Tragically, his dreams were crippled by the evils of his time, which refused him educational options as a Black man in Arkansas.

As a veteran of World War II, I think about the pain he carried to his grave. Here was a man, intelligent and full of capacity to accomplish great things, yet he was disallowed because of the color of his skin. Up to his last days on earth, my granddaddy reminded me of America's wrongs. He encouraged me to make things right. He critically analyzed President George W. Bush years, insisting that I know more of the political landscape for our people. I hurt thinking about my granddaddy's last days and all that was not materialized for his life despite his patriotic contribution to this, his country. How could a man stand up and fight in a war for his country while having this same country refuse to fight for him? I cringe at times thinking about his inability yet strong desire to break those chains of injustice.

As with Granddaddy, my dad passed away at the hands of unnecessary pain. What is there to say about a country that will literally work you to death? With no health insurance, my daddy died while at work. Having not been paid for overtime, no sick or vacation days, my dad worked until his last breath. Somewhat refreshing is the reality in knowing Daddy truly loved working in the field of maintenance. Oddly though, his passion as a youngster was ministry. As was the case of my granddaddy, Daddy's calling was arguably hijacked by a racist and abusive society. He would never realize his dream as priest and he settled in a field that allowed his superior work ethic.

I argue that the depth of societal ills such as racism, sexism, oppression, segregation, injustice and wickedness have been watered down and ignored. The pains associated with these evils are major. Consider an institution like slavery that debatably demanded of the slave the opposite of what God asked. All of what slavery forced upon us as a people contradicted the very calling God had for us as His children. Imagine a system so powerful it trumped God's purpose and presence. How could we not call it a satanic sin? What else is at work with such dominance? Over and over again, slaves were taught that White people were superior while being forced to live as inferior. This system of inferiority remained stained in America's fabric throughout the years causing the obvious pain in our communities to date.

Sure it is hard for many to grasp this as truth. We have been taught to live as inferior while at times questioning our ultimate Superior. Like the slave, our pain has resulted in various questions about our existence in the midst of such evil. Clearly, it is rather challenging to stand tall when being forced to lie on the ground with someone's foot on your neck. Where is God? Why have we endured such malicious behavior against us simply based on how God created us?

Many believe it is our disobedience to God and our current lack of faith that keeps us bound and now chained at times to iniquity. Obviously, this pain inflicted on our people over the years has caused insurmountable suffering. No other ethnic group can relate to this level of denial and rejection. Many argue that Blacks are just "lazy" wanting a handout. I immediately consider the handouts given on the plantation as we worked effortlessly for free. How lazy were Africans at that moment and honestly who really received handouts? Honestly, America and its anti-Black attitude abused an entire group of people while yet expecting that same group later to forgive by forgetting.

From the plantation of pain enters then the segregation stain. Over and over again, Blacks during the Civil Rights Movement were reminded of their imposed inferior status. Never were Blacks given a leveled playing field. Consequently, battles brewed in all parts of the country. In fact, it is important to mention here that it was not just a southern issue, this problem of racism and discrimination. Rev. Dr. Martin Luther King, Jr., having moved to Chicago to fight even the wickedness of the North declared that, "I've been in many demonstrations all across the South, but I can say that I had never seen, even in Mississippi, mobs as hostile and as hate-filled as in Chicago." (p. 305- *The Autobiography of Martin Luther King, Jr.,* 1998)

Dr. King, while protesting and marching in Chicago, said:

> Bottles and bricks were thrown at us; we were often
> beaten. Some of the people who had been brutalized in
> Selma and who were present at the Capitol ceremonies in
> Montgomery led marches in the suburbs of Chicago amid
> a rain of rocks and bottles, among burning automobiles,
> to the thunder of jeering thousands, many of them waving
> Nazi flags. Swastikas bloomed in Chicago parks like
> misbegotten weeds. Our marchers were met by a hailstorm
> of bricks, bottles, and firecrackers. 'White Power' became
> the racist catcall, punctuated by the vilest of obscenities
> ---most frequently directly at Catholic priests and nuns
> among the marchers. (p. 305)

So then, imagine the pain of Black folk all over the country still fighting
for freedom decades after the emancipation decreed by President Lincoln.
Constantly, there has existed the painful reminder of being told "no," just
because we are Black. Accordingly, the challenge is to still look beyond the
physical yet declaring that God is real and greater than what our conditions
may say to us. The chains of pain beginning on the plantation have resonated
like constant ocean waves throughout our generations. This pain is seen in
the eyes and felt from the hearts of many of us who respond in severe ways.
It is pain that often drives division in our families and runs daddy away from
home. It is this pain that cripples our children and youth. It is that same pain
through the years that has caused many to turn from victory to victim. This
pain that registers itself on the social networking site of our failures refuses to
accept God as a "friend" for our needed success.

So where is God? How about where is our faith in God? The lack of faith in our communities has sometime spun from religious bigotry and hypocrisy. Religion has been shoved down the throats of our people as an organic meal of deception while authentically choking us to death. Much of our faith has waned because of the chains of pain. The best answer for this is found in a sound relationship with God. This is our best solution. Religion does not denote relationship. Whether Christian, Muslim, Catholic, Jehovah Witness, or Jewish, the title does not speak to the total. The totality of where we are to be is found in how well we know God personally.

The crisis before us is magnified when we insist on calling ourselves in label what we deny in character. This is seen on a national level as our country proclaims itself a Christian nation while refusing Christ-like characteristics. The arrogant attributes demonstrated by many of us as Americans are hardly aligned to the character of Jesus. On many accounts, we have unfortunately adopted this attribute. Individually, we say in speech what those around us cannot see at work in our lives. God does not need a religious introduction in title; he desires a relationship in total. Our chains of pain then, be it molestation, rape, neglect, abuse, etc., are individual elements we must first rectify with our Creator who gives us new mercies each day. As God has kept us through the years despite the sin and setbacks of racist behavior toward us, too God will keep you through your personal chains of pain and infliction. Only when we declare to personally recognize our own pain, might we as a people transcend the communal pain we now see in our youth. In other words, we must first invoke healing in our lives via our personal relationship with God.

We must have a "no more" attitude with things. If daddy abused mommy and other women and you find yourself doing just that, you must declare, "no more!" If momma chose men over mothering her own children and you find yourself doing the same thing, you must declare, "no more!" When you find yourself reaching for a drink or unable to curtail your profane language in front of your children, doing what was done while you were their age, you must insist, "no more!" Why "no more"? Well, it is our "no more" attitude that will lessen the problems in our families and ultimately our communities. It is "no more" that will derail not all of the effects of racism at once, but how we acknowledge what racism has done and does. "No more" mis-educating and mis-informing stereotypically the genius of African folk worldwide. "No more" cheating our children of their history, denying them of their inherent power and purpose in life. We need healing for our youth that are now murdering each other at all time highs and overwhelmingly reading and studying at all time lows; to this we declare, "No More!"

A RELIGION THAT SOLELY SAVES ENSLAVES!

The Black church has long been a refuge for Black people. In the midst of crisis, it has been the Black church opting to function as an escape center for individuals dealing with day-to-day problems. Many people attending church seek support and encouragement. They are looking for a word from God. I often say we cannot look for this word in church when we have not prayed for it at home. Nonetheless, the church has served as an invaluable meeting place of worship and fellowship. Despite such, one of the greatest areas of criticism in the Black community is that of the church. Admittedly, this is a two-edged sword for the author. To say that the Black church has failed is a somewhat dubious position to take. Were it not for the church, I realize I would not be who and what I have become today. So what of this place, this building, this ministry warrants so much criticism and disappointment?

From where I sit, the church has produced large successes through the years. Despite all of its questioned doctrine, there was the church serving as a meeting ground for strategizing sessions and prayer for our people. It was the church that symbolized the power of God at work in us when society just did not work for us. It was the church that we owned and operated without large interference to handle the business at hand. Yet, today the Black church is at the center of great ridicule. The Black pastor is often viewed as the prophet that profits. Often, the many arguments of resentment deal with areas of social neglect. The unmet needs of our people financially, economically and educationally seem to war against churches and their often-criticized, heavenly focused doctrine. Who do I speak of in mentioning "the Black church"? It is the leadership of the church and the members within. Specifically, I chime in on the "Body of Christ" declaring Jesus as Lord.

In the New Testament of the Bible, chapter two of the book of Mark, you find these words:

> **1** A few days later, when Jesus again entered Capernaum, the people heard that he had come home. **2** So many gathered that there was no room left, not even outside the door, and he preached the word to them. **3** Some men came, bringing to him a paralytic, carried by four of them. **4** Since they could not get him to Jesus because of the crowd, they made an opening in the roof above Jesus and, after digging through it, lowered the mat the paralyzed man was lying on. **5** When Jesus saw their faith, he said to the paralytic, "Son, your sins are forgiven." **6** Now some teachers of the law were sitting there, thinking to themselves, **7** "Why does this fellow talk like that? He's blaspheming! Who can forgive sins but God alone?"

> **8** Immediately Jesus knew in his spirit that this was what they were thinking in their hearts, and he said to them, "Why are you thinking these things? **9** Which is easier: to say to the paralytic, 'Your sins are forgiven,' or to say, 'Get up, take your mat and walk'? **10** But that you may know that the Son of Man has authority on earth to forgive sins, He said to the paralytic, **11** "I tell you, get up, take your mat and go home."

For many, Jesus and the Bible have been tampered with, to say the least. Still, there are those who declare that, irrespective of these claims, their faith is in a God that will soon "save" them as He saved Jesus from death. Ultimately, this section is not a familiar attack on this doctrine of Jesus, but more of a critique on how He has been presented to Black folk.

In the above scripture there are many things happening. However, we see the actions of men in (v.3) and thus the action Jesus demonstrated because of their faith (v.5). The operative terminology here is *action*! What actions have we taken to save ourselves as Jesus saves? Sure, there is ultimate value in being saved. I immediately think of one drowning and needing to be rescued; the beauty of a lifeguard at that moment is splendid. I think of one trapped in a building enflamed with fire; the beauty of a firefighter at that moment is magnificent. Then, there is the one entrapped by sin needing grace and mercy; the beauty of a merciful God is glorious. Yes, the reality of needing to be saved and being rescued is unmatched.

However, I insist that, once saved from those drowning waters, an enflamed building or fiery trials, there is a work to be done — an action to take. Jesus was in action in the text, preaching the word of God to the people. The place was packed because of his track record as a healer. He was in high demand, so much so, you have these men in action, bringing their friend to him. Action is written all over this scripture. The profundity of the text is found in how Jesus took action forgiving the man's sins (v.5) and then providing him with an ability to walk (v.11). Jesus, in healing the man's soul, dared to take action in favor of his body. Thus, there is a prophetic word in this classic moment. Jesus refused to ignore the man's spiritual need and dared to satisfy his physical state of being.

This is important to the Black church as an institution that "saves." Undoubtedly, other religions and denominations beyond the "Body of

Christ" warrant such critique as well. Yet, specific to the criticism of having a church on every urban block, there is room for a fair analysis.

It is time we look at how we look. It is imperative that we critique a doctrine that "saves." In this I do not intend to ultimately and theologically agitate the lens of salvation, for in the end we shall all see God. In this I mean that salvation, in its deepest sense, connects us to God who grants us reprieve for our sins. What more does God care for us to have, considering the text? Was it only about our soul and nothing more as we wither away awaiting heaven? I think not. In fact, I suggest that such teaching is centered on further enslavement and spiritual detention.

The Christian faith in America has meant much to a people simply wanting to be whole. This idea of being whole for so many today in urban communities translates into a matter of the soul plus justice, perhaps some fairness in hiring, equity in schools and equality in the political process. Being "saved" has become an unwarranted joke because of how Jesus has been portrayed. Ultimately, the argument is in how we have offered salvation through the lens of being "saved" and nothing more. This doctrine enslaves. If all we were commissioned to be was "saved," as many of us have learned traditionally, then how could we carry out the great commission? Note what Jesus said in the book of Matthew, chapter 28:

> **16** Then the eleven disciples went to Galilee, to the mountain where Jesus had told them to go. **17** When they saw him, they worshiped him; but some doubted. **18** Then Jesus came to them and said, "All authority in heaven and on earth has been given to me. **19** Therefore go and make disciples of all nations, baptizing them in the name of the Father and of the Son and of the Holy Spirit, **20** and

teaching them to obey everything I have commanded you. And surely I am with you always, to the very end of the age."

This great commission, as expressed by our Savior, includes the action word "go." Our religious beliefs must take action against enslavement. We must move and go as Jesus commanded rightfully in this great commission. Jesus was able to instruct the disciples as such because of what he did throughout his ministry. Note one last time, how he could have solely "saved" the soul of the man brought to him, yet he proved to those arguing his authority, his power as he empowered the man physically. The subliminal parallel is found in how we must go and move with an action agenda of saving ourselves from lowly living, doubtful doing and blatant bigotry. All in all, salvation offers amongst many things, faith; and in this faith as expressed in the book of Hebrews 11:3, "we understand that the entire universe was formed at God's command, that what we now see did not come from anything that can be seen."

All in all, our limitations are made clear by the One who really "saves." Notwithstanding though is our necessary work as His children made in His image. Any religion that promotes being "saved" void of a work to do is debatably disconnected from a sound relationship with our Most High God.God is not passive; He is a God of action. In that, we must analyze our activity as His children. Perhaps we will find a connection to our passivity and our enslavement. The tragedy for so many within our culture, is found in our passive patience. However, the time is now for us to act on what it means to be "saved," beyond your comfortable and traditional teachings of waiting.

Remember now, the brothers took their guy to see Jesus for their healing; they did not wait on Jesus to come and save them.

I HAVE ONE QUESTION PASTOR,
IS THE TRUTH RESERVED
FOR JUDGMENT DAY ONLY?

I must say what I heard a pastor say long ago, "The church hasn't failed, as it is what saved me." Like that preacher, I must admit that the church, particularly the Black church, hasn't failed in totality as it truly "saved" me. This institution is pertinent to this chapter and my manuscript overall. Here I expound on my testimony in that the church, as a building of "Believers," helped me in my walk with God. I, like Christopher Columbus, ran into many people whom I happened to like and whom I, unlike Columbus, assimilated with, well, more or less. I often wonder what would have happened had that same Christopher Columbus discovered the Black church? Would this quoted preacher have the luxury of testifying to a real faith had it been hijacked and never seen? (Some faith that would be.) Wow. My point here, though, is the number of those within the Christian faith who question aspects of the faith and, in so doing, are left feeling like hell, that hot place, is their destiny. How is this so? Why is this so? Are not questions good for the soul? And are not answers the launching pad for healing? Biblically, I learned that Jesus came as the way, the truth and the light. This truth, if of Jesus, clearly signifies some form or element of what we should seek.

The "it matters not attitude" is simply unacceptable for crucial questions. "We have not, because we ask not" rings aloud in the minds of many. Matthew 7:7 suggests, "Seek and ye shall find." So what is wrong with questioning Jesus' true race? Is it blasphemous to inquire of those lost books in the Bible and how this impacts one's overall belief system? Now,

I do understand what is at the heart of such responses centered on what matters most. I hear the positions clearly on the Spirit of man and those that lie, for instance, someday being accountable for their sin(s) before God. I raise this point, though; Will we experience truth only on Judgment Day? Yes, I believe we will all someday find ourselves before God and accountable to Him. I also believe that this accountability starts with my walk here on earth. The very Judgment we will have is in critique of our lives here. Thus, I am required to do the best I can as a "Believer" while here. This includes, as the Bible suggests, identification of the false prophets seeking to dissemble the truth.

To those with questions on the matter, I recognize that truth is very subjective and relative. I know too though that truth does exist. The truth is found in slavery being real. It is true that Black people could not read as slaves, as illiteracy was encouraged legally. It is also true that the same man-made laws that encouraged illiteracy made it legal to lynch Blacks. Are these facts, and other truths, irrelevant or just relative and subjective? Why withhold such historical truths? Far too many churches dance around relevant topics for Blacks in America. I once heard, "If I feed a homeless man, I am considered a saint. If I ask why he is homeless, I am communist." It appears that as American citizens we have comfort in what we do not know because the "truth hurts." Whatever happened to "no pain, no gain"? If we are to experience growth in this country and in our communities it begins with truth as relevant.

Youth today have questions regarding their realities. Answers exist. We cannot afford to choke their questions while lies breathe. To not have an answer is one thing, but to misinform someone is something else. Moreover, to misguide one's soul in the name of The Truth, albeit a lie, is unacceptable and detrimental. We must see the connection. If God is truth and we are made in His image, then inherently we (should) desire such truth. The challenge in understanding all of it is found in how so many lies have been offered up as truth. Blacks have for too long been bamboozled in this capacity. The Tuskegee Syphilis Experiment is a great example of such.

Three hundred and ninety-nine Black men living with syphilis were enlisted as part of a scientific study. The aim was to track and research the natural progression of the disease with eventual hopes of justifying treatment programs for Blacks. The men were told at the onset of the study that they were to be tested for "bad blood." In exchange for their participation, they received free food, free medical examinations and free burial insurance. The study initially set to last for six months lasted forty years. Forty years! This is not the 1800's during slavery, by the way. It began in 1932 and lasted until 1972. Despite an emerging and existent cure in penicillin during the former years of the study, this information was withheld from the subjects. After a leak regarding the unethical behavior of the scientists, a lawsuit was filed on behalf of the participants and their families in 1973. A settlement was reached for $10,000,000. Again, it is important to mention that this study lasted 40 years! It was conducted on behalf of the United States Public Health Service. Several participants later died from syphilis, despite the newfound cure of penicillin. This evil act committed against Blacks as subjects for science further validates a long history of Black folks' mistrust of government, science, doctors and public health.

Dr. John Heller, Director of the Public Health Service's Division of Venereal Disease, later stated, "For the most part, doctors and civil servants simply did their jobs. Some merely followed orders, others worked for the glory of science."

I suggest that simply doing "their job" entailed lying to those involved for the sake of achieving a desired outcome that callously rejected Black life as human. Such thinking permeates the minds of many. Further, the lies told constantly and over time are not irrelevant nor are they merely old news. Such lies cause actual death as witnessed in this experiment. Over and over again, we find incomplete stories and untold truths.

The lie of Black folk being lazy, unfit and uncaring is inconsistent with those hard working Blacks who cared enough to leave behind their inventions we so utilize every day. Those unfit Black mothers as slaves nurtured the babies of their slave owners, feeding and clothing them daily. Jesus' resurrection occurred on a particular day, did it not? Which part of the world? Was it in March or April or is it subjective and connected to what we feel works best for our calendar year? Is it, in fact, real?

These are all pertinent questions for many of our youth and those inquiring. Seeking such is not blasphemous; it is the denying of such that is out of order, spiritually. For the pastor and the Spiritual leadership of our times, truth should not stand trial with a biased jury set on its conviction. The truth of the matter is this: the time is now to cross examine those defending falsehood in protection of their own interest and the Judge finds them guilty on all counts.

-THREE-

◇✕◇

[Black Community]

Photo courtesy of Jamel Shabazz

Arrogant Ignorance [39]
and Ignorant Arrogance

"Girl, something is wrong with you, ain't nothing wrong with meat;
you just don't know what you're missing." These words are often spoken
from the mouths of many who hear of my chosen lifestyle as a vegan. As
a vegan I do not eat any meat, poultry, fish, seafood, etc. Nor do I
consume dairy products such as eggs, milk and cheese. As a vegan I, in
summary, do not eat the animal nor do I consume that of what comes
from it, i.e., not even milk chocolate. This has been my lifestyle for seven
years now. I was once a size 20 and weighed over 200 pounds. With my
medical condition and necessary medication to be consumed daily, I was
plagued with weight issues early in my adolescent years. After each doctor's
visit, it became the norm to discuss possible diets. One of the side effects
of my medication was weight gain and, as a young girl, I was reminded
more and more of my being overweight. In thinking back on this, I recall
the brushed off pain in hearing the doctor often reference the need for
my weight loss. I would soon learn that my issue was not solely the side
effects; it was also my love for candy, cookies and potato chips.

Growing up in inner-city communities, can be hazardous to one's
health. The consumption of junk food is normal. This is not endemic only
to Black communities and inner-city areas; I know of few children who
wouldn't choose cookies over an apple. In fact, America, as the most obese
country, thrives on junk food eating with few boundaries. Fast food restaurants reign as popular and good tasting dinner options. More times than
none fried foods accompany large greasy burgers with cheese, bacon,

sauces and two to three pieces of bread. Adding a large soda with a dessert yields us more calories in that one sitting than the recommended intake for nearly two days.

So, how do you give up what tastes so good to you? Why give up what tastes so good to you? What is the benefit of eating better? Besides, "we all have to die from something." Yes, we will all die from something, but shall we choose how to die? Why not live? Diseases in America are amongst the worse in the world. Weight is a major issue. Far too many of our children are overweight and simply not active. Inner-city communities suffer most. It is no secret that this issue largely affects Black folk. Hypertension, heart disease, diabetes, cancer, etc., all plague our communities at alarming rates. Early detection would, of course, resolve some of these as problems yet many live without medical insurance and others opt out of visiting and trusting doctors.

Most relevant, however, is our desire to live. Can we eliminate from our diets cultural norms and habits such as bags of chips for breakfast, fast food for lunch and candy bars for dinner? Are we willing to live? Are we willing to change and grow? A better question is, what is it that you want out of life? Far too many of us live in fear. It is fear that drives our decisions. It is fear that keeps us from making better decisions. It is fear that all too often guides us in our lives. It is that same fear that speaks through what I call arrogant ignorance and ignorant arrogance.

Arrogance is a sense of overbearing pride and self-importance. It bears an assuming superiority in that you feel greater, better and larger than most. Ignorance in this context is that of what you do not know. It is a lack of knowledge and information. In putting these two together, I have concluded that we are sadly comfortable with that of what we do not know. Not only so, we exude a level of arrogance as if ignorance is okay.

We are strangely content and often cocky about our levels of ignorance.

In finding out certain foods are not good for our overall health, we insist that we have "to die from something." When learning "you are what you eat," we continue to eat as we have been raised to eat. We then validate such foolishness with responses connected to how our mothers and grandmothers lived "to be 80 and she ate this way." Ignorance does not know, and arrogance is being okay with what you do not know. This is an unfortunate prideful state of being. If I suggest to you that over 90% of those with lung cancer are or were themselves smokers, would you stop? How about a recommendation of eliminating soda and candies from your diet, as they are heavy in sugar? Would you give them up? The point is that we are reckless in our decision-making. We have made a life of not caring about what we do not know and we have made a living from not caring enough to change what it is we do know. All the more devastating is that we do not desire to change when we do find out the truth. Underneath this is a prideful fear that we possess.

See, it is fear that guides this arrogant ignorance and ignorant arrogance. It is fear that keeps us in a comfort zone even though in the end we are poor, unhealthy and uncomfortable. Nelson Mandela suggests this:

> Our deepest fear is not that we are inadequate. Our deepest fear is that we are powerful beyond measure. It is our light, not our darkness that most frightens us. We ask ourselves, Who am I to be brilliant, gorgeous, talented, fabulous? Actually, who are you not to be? You are a child of God. Your playing small does not serve the world. There is nothing enlightened about shrinking so that other people won't feel insecure around you. We are

all meant to shine, as children do. We were born to make manifest the glory of God that is within us. It's not just in some of us; it's in everyone. And as we let our own light shine, we unconsciously give other people permission to do the same. As we are liberated from our own fear, our presence automatically liberates others.

Blackademically Speaking, Fear Kills! Arrogance is unhealthy and ignorance is just ignorant! If we hear that "All that is good is not good for us," we must decide individually to change our ways. We must digest and consume healthy choices as our lifestyle. This is not simply specific to food, albeit that is our greatest example here. Choosing to serve heart attacks on your plate is as hazardous as drinking diabetes. The fact of the matter is that, no, we cannot avoid all ailments and disease. However, I insist that we can prevent many of these inflictions. Yes, you can probably live a life as long as your grandparents, but why roll the dice eating anything? Grandma and Grandpa didn't have to battle such a polluted environment, AIDS, crack cocaine and street violence. Today, too many odds are already stacked against us. God's grace is capable of giving you life, but discipline and better decisions gives you a long *healthy* life. In fear we trust! Is this your life motto? If not, welcome to living and not dying because we all have to *live* for something.

MOLESTED DREAMS

Okay, now remember that this is one big secret meaning you cannot tell anyone. This is our secret. What I do with you is no different than what I will do to you. Now, just for a moment I need your undivided attention as I hypnotize you. It will only take a moment and before you know it things will be back to normal again. Listen reeeeeal well and close your eyes. Take deep breaths and focus on sleeping. As you focus on sleeping, think of something you love, somewhere you wish you were at this moment in time. Is it an island? How about your favorite vacation spot? Focus and breathe. Okay, can you hear me? Are you asleep? Perfect!

Now that you are asleep, I wish to remind you of your past. I am a dream that is no dream at all. In fact, I come as your current reality in the form of a dream. I am here to illustrate what your life is and who exactly is in your life. Do you feel violated? Do you feel vulnerable? Are you very sad and hurt by what they managed to get away with? What did they tell you to not say to anyone? Did you believe them? How did they touch you? Where did they harm you? How long ago was it? Was it your father, mother, auntie, uncle or cousin? Perhaps it was no one in your family but a "very close friend" of the family. Maybe it was mom's boyfriend or daddy's girlfriend. Or perhaps they just raped you in the name of loving you.

Wait, don't wake up, I have some things to reveal to you; give me just a few more moments. You see, in your innocence, as a child there existed some immature and wicked people. Having not overcome their own issues, they passed down their evil ways. Within them are sinful spirits that attempt to attack us all. You are not alone as the victim nor are they alone as predators. There are many in the world that produces such madness and badness. Likewise, there are many in the world having fallen victim to this sadness. Your sadness must be addressed. It is you that must break the generational curse. Many can be saved if you believe in the power of your situation. This may sound crazy but trust that it is not. Remember my legal situation that produced the felony?

Well, my dream to be a Ph.D. was nearly deferred. I believe people who possessed this very spirit of "badness" molested my dreams then.

Waaaake up! Waaake up! Can you hear me? Coooome back!

Hold on, before you leave me I must tell you that your dreams of becoming great are intricately connected to the not-so-great moments you have experienced. That's right, I said it! You see, my felony was unnecessary in that no one should have to endure the evil inflicted upon humankind because of those that are unkind. However, I contend that the felony was necessary only in that it shows the apparent and existent evils of the legal system. It highlights how cops having a bad day or just bad ways can molest dreams. It portrays via necessity the unjust power of the predator and the vulnerability of the victim. It helps to expose how evil becomes innocent of its own crimes while not serving any time.

So then, this person molesting you is wrong despite what they say. You are innocent and must reveal the truth. As you leave this state of hypnosis, remember this was your reality posing as a dream. Sometimes dreams aim to reveal things to you. Take heed and believe in your own power to change your predicament. The person having you under their spell believed they exercised some power in putting you to sleep just now. Yet, like the individual who put their filthy hands on you, this hypnosis was your wake-up call to alert you. It was not about putting you to sleep after all. One great hip-hop artist, the pioneering female rapper MC Lyte, said in a song years ago:

The grace as I ease across the stage
Bars around the audience, sort of like a cage
They laugh, 'cause they assume I'm in prison
But in reality, they're locked in.

Your quality of life now depends on you and your ability to move beyond the prison of your problems. Unfortunately, there exist too many people who prey on the bodies and even the minds of folk like you. They laugh, because they assume you are in prison but, in reality, they're locked inside. It is now about perspective; it is time you change the way you see what happened to you. If it is happening to you now, it is time you escape trusting in your ultimate Judge. Do not believe the one desiring to lull you to sleep. Do not trust the one desiring to molest you, thus molesting your dreams. They are locked in their prison of being predators. They seek to cage your life, and it is now time for you to utilize these keys to unlock yourself from bondage.

First, know that there is a true Judge waiting to hear your case. In God's royal court, you can present your arguments of defense. This is done in prayer. After prayer feel free to deliberate with the Holy Spirit consulting the Bible for your supporting cases. Lastly, know that you are God's chosen vessel and anyone putting his or her hands on you in any inappropriate manner really violates God. God shall have the last word with them. You must begin your state of healing as God delivers you from the hands of this wickedness. One last thing, before you leave me and go back to your awakened state, do not allow your teacher, counselor, a family member or any so-called friend to molest your dreams. Seek to be the very best you can as God elevates you. Learn more of those who have experienced God first-hand and allow that to be your blueprint for moving on in your life.

I introduce you to the Apostle Paul who wrote 20% of the entire Bible and 50% of the New Testament. It is God that changed Paul's life. It was Paul (then known as Saul) who abused and murdered those believing in the ministry of Jesus. If God can forgive and use Paul as "a chosen instrument," imagine what He has in store for you. In the book of Acts, chapter nine you have these words:

> Meanwhile, Saul was uttering threats with every breath and was eager to kill the Lord's followers. So he went to the high priest. **2** He requested letters addressed to the synagogues in Damascus, asking for their cooperation in the arrest of any followers of the Way he found there. He wanted to bring them-both men and women-back to Jerusalem in chains. **3** As he was approaching Damascus on this mission, a light from heaven suddenly shone down around him. **4** He fell to the ground and heard a voice saying to him, "Saul! Saul! Why are you persecuting me?" **5** "Who are you, lord?" Saul asked. And the voice replied, "I am Jesus, the one you are persecuting! **6** Now get up and go into the city, and you will be told what you must do." **7** The men with Saul stood speechless, for they heard the sound of someone's voice but saw no one! **8** Saul picked himself up off the

ground, but when he opened his eyes he was blind. So his companions led him by the hand to Damascus. **9** He remained there blind for three days and did not eat or drink. **10** Now there was a believer in Damascus named Ananias. The Lord spoke to him in a vision, calling, "Ananias!" "Yes, Lord!" he replied. **11** The Lord said, "Go over to Straight Street, to the house of Judas. When you get there, ask for a man from Tarsus named Saul. He is praying to me right now. **12** I have shown him a vision of a man named Ananias coming in and laying hands on him so he can see again." **13** "But Lord," exclaimed Ananias, "I've heard many people talk about the terrible things this man has done to the believers in Jerusalem! **14** And he is authorized by the leading priests to arrest everyone who calls upon your name." **15** But the Lord said, "Go, for Saul is my chosen instrument to take my message to the Gentiles and to kings, as well as to the people of Israel. **16** And I will show him how much he must suffer for my name's sake." **17** So Ananias went and found Saul. He laid his hands on him and said, "Brother Saul, the Lord Jesus, who appeared to you on the road, has sent me so that you might regain your sight and be filled with the Holy Spirit." **18** Instantly something like scales fell from Saul's eyes, and he regained his sight. Then he got up and was baptized.

It is now time for you to instantly address your situation. It is now time for you to get up! Remember those keys we discussed earlier. Most challenging in all of this is for you to forgive the predator in your life. In so doing, you release him or her into the hands of God and as God changed Saul (the predator) into Paul, so, too, can He deal with one who has hurt you. Holding onto the pain of this problem imprisons you and further cripples your life. Let them go; do not allow your molested dreams to rape you of the greatness God has planned for you.

The tampering with your innocence is not just that of your body but an unfortunate touching and tampering with the very dreams you have for your life and that of what GOD has in store for you...the delicate dreams connected with your purpose.

POVERTY AIN'T NO PUNK —ASK JESUS

Here I draw off the urban vernacular of said streets, the block and those corners that I have mentioned thus far. "No punk," for clarity, implies it is beyond difficult living, as Dr. King suggested, amidst "a sea of wealth" when one either has none of it or limited access to it.

Ideally, for me, public universities like public elementary and high schools, would be free. The mere fact that schools are no longer free post high school leads me to the discussion on who's entitled to this education we speak so eloquently of in America. *For me,* growing up "in the 'hood" simply "ain't no punk." Abandoned buildings and vacant lots are intricately connected to the abandoned children and vacant thinking. Coupled with a church almost always being across the street from the liquor store owned often by Arabs, it's hard to feel God as One who would allow such hypocrisy.

For me, it is often hard to just blame young men and women growing up in such harsh conditions. Consider this: we had one basketball court in my entire neighborhood on the south side of Chicago. There were no community centers, enrichment programs were scarce and unspoken of, and one public library with outdated books. Others in my community were notorious for making up games like "pitching pennies," "off the wall" and "It." We had no choice. As a young athlete, considering our one basketball court, one of the favorite pastimes was the makeshift rim nailed to trees.

Poverty somehow brought out the best in these children. Like street legends on basketball courts that never graduated high school, too much of the genius of Black children is underdeveloped, incarcerated, or buried six feet under. Daily games were invented with subconscious attempts to stay active and free from trouble. All that was needed for these makeshift rims was a crate (literally), a hard, wooden, flat board, nails, a hammer (or anything comparable), a good longstanding tree and healthy bodies. The crate was broken and beaten until both ends were pulled. Once achieved, two people were responsible for climbing the tree (rarely were we able to locate a ladder to achieve this step). After carrying the crate to the tree, the tool was passed with the nails. The board was first nailed to the tree. Afterwards, the crate was nailed to the board. As you might wonder, this was a remarkably tedious process, often resulting in a crooked "rim."

As a young academician, Blackademically Speaking, I supply you with this:

> The parallel of who Christ is to many starts and ends
> with what he did on the cross.
>> His blood - - - - Their nails.
>> His courage - - - - - Their laws.
>> His death - - - - - - - My life.

Well, safe to say it was nails for the masses metaphorically that saved many from death in "the 'hood." Simply put, it was nails that connected the bottomless crate to the tree. This makeshift hoop became an outlet for many staying out of trouble. It was these nails that gave street legends hope and impoverished children something to do. These nails strengthened relationships as it was a game of horse or 3-on-3 that helped pass the time on this makeshift rim and court, which more times than none kept youth away from the bloody summers so many spoke of and even witnessed year after year.

By no means is this parallel a disrespectful hit to a functioning faith. It is merely a window by way to view what I call an urban salvation. Nailed to the cross was Jesus — this produced blood for religious salvation. Nailed to the tree were these crates — this reduced blood, thus urban salvation.

From this makeshift rim to the monkey bars, basketball was a commonly loved sport with universal mechanisms in playing it. Interestingly, this sport produced in many communities what was called "street legends." For those of us growing up in similar elements, these individuals were the best to play the game. They were talented beyond measure. Their "game" was competitive, strong and they would just dominate in various facets of local tournaments, 1-on-1's and many pickups. Their competitiveness somehow could not reach beyond the court into classrooms. This is incredibly essential to my point here. What made them "street legends" were the realities that again were brushed over in day-to-day conversations. Many had not finished high school and, if so, their college careers were ended almost at first thought. Some would fault their low achieving status throughout elementary and high school. Others who understood the game would attribute their lack to an inability to play the sport as a team, learning fundamentals and other components essential to their overall development in the game. Amazingly, this is critical because much of their natural talent proved to be underdeveloped because of lack of resources on various levels. Further, their attitudes about life in general impeded their own growth on and off the court.

Let me say that poverty itself is not the sole reason for life as it is for so many youth in inner cities. Quite the contrary, as there are many who find their way in life, successfully and quite determined to achieve. Yet it is extremely important to highlight how poverty kills, literally.

- FOUR -

〈〉〈〉

[Black Children | Youth]

Photo courtesy of Jamel Shabazz

IN IT AND NOT OF IT!

Admittedly, many of those "street legends" referenced here from my vantage point were skilled ironically because of their own genius. Many will challenge this, but the two edged sword to this issue of not having is a precarious creativity that is born. Learning how to shoot on crates, or monkey bars is indeed humbling. Moreover, so is the imaginative, ingenious and inventive spirit of youth when given few resources. Truthfully, the history of Blacks in America has been such. I have heard many elders say countless times that they did not know they were poor. I find this to be quite astounding and honestly still question the totality of such. How can you NOT know you are poor when you have few clothes, little food and short change, literally? Nonetheless, one direct reason I have attributed to such thinking is how families maintained a sense of virtue despite their lack. Parents instilled in their children the need to "walk with your head high," "treat people how you wanna be treated," and the most infamous statement made with finger(s) pointed at one's head in regards to education, "get this, because if you get this, they can't take it way from you."

Somehow, from the shores in chains to segregated lunch counters, Black folks maintained an intense level of respect for education and its importance. It is estimated that over 85% of Blacks emerged from slavery illiterate, and yet they insisted upon educating themselves despite laws and a society that perpetually relegated them to inferior roles. Resilience helped us emerge as brilliant and, at times, dominant. Unfortunately, poverty is no new thing for many Black people. Being denied jobs, housing and even college admission based on race, are mere examples of America's longstanding mistreatment of Blacks. Notwithstanding this, are the side effects of poverty today, which include hopelessness, crime, health and educational disparities, apathy, underachievement, drugs, gangs, etc. These side effects invariably lead to nominal success. Thus poverty is vicious on so many levels. Despite differences in thought amongst our elders who knew not their poverty, it is incredibly awkward being forced to forego tangible wealth because of limited options and resources.

What is the difference between an impoverished mind and an impoverished man? Are they not one in the same? Well here, as learned by our elders, you can be in it and not of it. In fact, in choosing to be not of it, your mind is free to dance with possibility despite an environment that insist on impossible. Sadly, though too many of our children are being asked to reach for the stars on cloudy nights. Besides, let's ask the Realist why a child is asked to just dream in such realities? It is not solely the dream of the child and an oppressed people that will take away the disease of poverty, albeit a good start. I submit that institutions and individuals should ultimately be accountable in creating realities consistent with our children's dreams.

MODERN-DAY MALCOLM SAGS HIS PANTS

Pointing to their head with their index finger, parents and neighbors alike insist that you "get this (education) because they can never take that away from you." Education and empowerment for Blacks has always been historically connected to social and even political uplift. When one achieved, the thinking was that all should benefit; thus, progress was never intended to be some selfish agenda, as the stakes were too high considering the many left behind. What one achieved, generally speaking, was a testament of hope and freedom for others. Blatant racism, legal discrimination and unjust poverty were obstacles in the way of true progress. When one could hurdle these obstacles, their potential for a bright career brought hope to so many more and their future as well. So what happened? How have we gone from hopefulness to helplessness? Of course it is important to note that, throughout generations, challenges have always persisted. However, we must agitate with this question: what is really going on?

Malcolm X, born Malcolm Little, is modern-day "Mike Mike" for me. You know, the brother who stands on the block, absent in mind and body from school and all things related. You know him wearing white tees and pants sagging nearly to the ground. This is not some bogus stereotype of men (and even women for that matter) who sag their pants. Albeit some will take offense, deeming this essay largely judgmental, I welcome such critique. Be it as unpopular as it may, this issue is an important one.

It is my position and critique that it is not the sag itself, but the thinking that often accompanies the sag. Ask yourself (or those young men you know), are you where God wants you to be right now, at this moment? Are you where you are supposed to be? You have been called to do a work, especially assigned to you; do you know what it is? For those few "well-established" saggers answering yes to all of these, I welcome you to share in the responsibility component of this. I ask you, have you considered the example you set for those young men unlike you striving to do as you do? I have seen accomplished young men who, having achieved much and become somewhat successful in their own right, persist in sagging their pants as well. The premise is simple. Far too many of our young men, having not achieved nor desiring to understand achievement, swear by the sag and other cultural chaos that keep them bound. For the few who opt to sag as individual empowerment, I welcome you on this road of assessment for the many who dress as you, yet proven nowhere near as successful as you.

There is a suffocating thinking keenly associated with the sag itself. The sag is not what promotes the thinking; it is the thinking that ignites the sag. For many of our youth today, it is the hanging on the street corner, the blunts, the drinking, and, of course, the sag. For me, it all represents and equals the demise of a generation. It is cultural chaos having emerged in our communities that is unchallenged and unchecked. The sagging for me, inclusive of analysis, is metaphoric and symbolic. It is the swag of the sag that I will use as my lens of empowerment for champions in the making.

The "swag" is urban terminology used in many communities to date. To have "swag" is to have style, it is your own flavor and fashion. It is an appeal. So then I ask, what "swag" is in the sag? Why the sag? Or, as my father would say, "Where is your belt?"

Malcolm X was one of the most misunderstood and misconstrued men in history. His lifestyle as a street hustler gives us a window by way to see through for understanding our younger brothers of today. Having initially missed his calling by God for the call of the streets, Malcolm insisted on the hustle, the game. As with young Malcolm, many of our youth (and adults for that matter) find themselves incarcerated mentally. I submit that these chains, spoken of largely in chapter one, make us unconscious and simply uncritical of our behavior and actions. So we begin to rationalize insanity with little regard for sanity. Our beloved Brother Malcolm X states:

> "Nobody can give you freedom. Nobody can give you equality or justice or anything. If you're a man, you take it."

Brother Malcolm suggests that men take their freedom! You don't wait on someone to give you what he or she may not want you to have. I suggest that in so doing it starts by, if nothing more, acknowledging the symbolism in pulling up your pants. Men who pull up their pants position themselves powerfully to themselves be lifted up. Lift up your pants and lift your thinking. There is no swag in the sag. The only potential swag is in your expression of individual freedom. How exhilarating is it really, in objecting to those who wrongfully stereotype you? Is that all you got? Your responses to express and rebel just because you can do whatever you feel you want to do and not care what others think? That's your best expression of individual freedom? Brothers and sisters I propose pulling your pants up as a new form of rebellion against being down. I propose lifting yourself up out of bondage and I encourage you to mentally attack ANYTHING that is down. Lift your head! Lift your fellow brothers and sisters! Lift your communities! Pull up your pants as you pull up your families.

Our brother Malcolm was lifted out of a lifestyle that could have eventually killed him. To my brothers, you are the new millennium Malcolm X! Malcolm X, despite popular thinking, was already intelligent and jail did not educate him academically. Jail was where he met a man that lifted him. He lifted him out of mental incarceration and later physical incarceration. Malcolm is quoted in his autobiography as speaking about his teacher Mr. Ostrowski who asked him what his ambition was in life. Having not much thought on the subject prior to, he says he stated what seemed great (to say). He replied, "An attorney." Mr. Ostrowski's posited that he should consider carpentry, as he seemed good with his hands. Mr. Ostrowski, a dream killer, saw little in Malcolm, yet Malcolm met a man who introduced him to One that lifts humanity.

The issue of the sag is not the pants. It's the lack of purpose often connected to it. It is the dignity and integrity that must be infused into this discussion. On a very basic level, it is cataclysmic in being okay with our elders having to see your underwear. This is a thinking that is cancerous. To ignore the disease does not mean you are not infected. To disregard the symptoms, only leads to a more hazardous state. To treat the problems is to heal. It is no questioning the healing needed for this cultural catastrophe we are witnessing. Let's lift our spirits and thus lift one another out of downtrodden, down thinking. What's down we don't want or need in our lives. We bury people six feet underground, that's down in the ground. When we have down days, we sometimes look down. We are not a down people. Look up, lift up and metaphorically speaking pull up your families, your thinking, your communities and yes your pants. I leave you with Malcolm and a few of his quotes:

- Without education, you are not going anywhere in this world.
- You can't legislate good will – that comes through education.
- You can't separate peace from freedom because no one can be at peace unless he has his freedom.
- You don't have to be a man to fight for freedom. All you have to do is be an intelligent human being.

SUICIDAL SANCTUARIES

Taking up residence in the depths of despair, so many of our youth are often accused of desiring nothing more than their existent, yet terrible conditions. This is insane for me considering the inhumane conditions of their environments. I believe Black youth are desperate for something greater, something better. However, with so little to live for, much of their minds, hearts and souls find it hard to grasp the unseen greatness of what life really has to offer. A lack of personal exposure to excellence, leads to a seemingly yet frustrated comfort with mediocrity. Too many of our children, having never left their neighborhood, are asked to see and conquer the world. They often see rims on cars and desire to be just as those who drive such cars. This is not the case for all of our youth. Yet, it is important to highlight what captures our children's attention in their homes, on television and in their neighborhoods.

Consider the connection between abandoned buildings in neighborhoods and abandoned children. Growing up near alleys is a rough experience, especially when there are more alleys than homes. I shake my head when I hear those on the outside criticizing and blaming those inside this reality. While we are entitled to our own thoughts and opinions, I caution those folk in their thinking and I challenge their mindset.

Simply, the sanctity of our youth is connected to arguably the three most important institutions in our communities. The school and the church are social and spiritual sanctuaries that should develop our youth. Who would argue against spiritual salvation and excellent education provided by the church and the school respectively and respectably? The challenge before our youth today, however, connects to their mind and heart as sanctuary. For some of our youth today, they have learned to not want to learn. They have been taught at their own demise how to accept abnormal conditions as normal and uncommon situations as common. Strangely, many find refuge in habit-forming addictions that push them further away from their divine purpose.

Yet, what shall I offer you, our youth, reading this? What is your sanctuary? What is your place of refuge? Do you feel safe or unsafe? How do you manage life when life seems unmanageable? My daddy was known for saying, "if life was easy, everyone would want to do it." For years I missed his point. I later learned that those who chose not to "do it" often lived coping and crying. The greatest people amongst us, however, find ways to live despite their circumstances. Fact is, life is not "easy." However, it is made easier as we trust God.

For many, life and all of its misfortunes pushes them to the edge. According to a recent study conducted in 2009 by the Substance Abuse and Mental Health Services Administration (SAMHSA), nearly 8.3 million adults (age 18 and older) in America had serious thoughts of suicide. The study also shows that 2.3 million adult Americans made a suicide plan in the past year and that 1.1 million adults actually attempted such in the past year.

Clearly, spirits of depression, anger, fear and frustration welcome suicidal thoughts. the sanctuary of a hopeful heart is critical in eliminating your desire to not live. As a teenager, things are all the more challenging as you seek to understand your personal growth and development, while witnessing an underdeveloped and non-growing community. Fret not; you are not alone! Your heart and mind as sanctuary must be at peace. As my daddy also said, light is not at the end of the tunnel as we have learned, light is throughout the tunnel. I have taken this to suggest that God is the light and He is always with us.

Earlier, I mentioned there were three institutions most important to our communities. The institution of family is of grave significance and always has been, specific to our plight here in America. Family is important to our personal and social development. We must note, what family means to some, is different for others. Still, there is power in what we have known as the traditional family—with mother and father. There is power in what many of us are familiar with as extended family, specifically, grandmothers, cousins, etc., as well. What happens when this power is seldom realized in the lives of our children? How do we proclaim this power when parents refuse to assume their roles as parents?

Please note, the absence of a parent does not automatically denote failure. Many women single-handedly raised their children successfully, particularly with the presence of extended family members and friends. Yet, few would argue in fairness the blessing of having a family with both mom and dad present. Fewer could argue the serious effects of being raised in a dysfunctional family. Make no mistake about it, having both parents present does not suggest wholeness. The greater good for any family, is for it to be functional, healthy and peaceful.

Have you ever thought about what your life would be with a stronger family connection? Do you spend time wondering about what it would mean to actually utter "daddy"? Some of you reading this may have never seen your daddy. Immediately after conceiving you, he left you. You may have tragically lost your mom. Perhaps you were a toddler and a car accident or cancer activated her demise. The bottom line is the absence of a parent, any parent, is not a game. Equally important too, is any breakdown in your family.

Many people struggle in life as a result of their dysfunctional family.

Regrettably, this is unrecognized in many of our communities. In other words, what is dysfunctional? The existence of drug addiction, alcoholism and abuse all aid in my reference to being dysfunctional. Imagine it being strange to live a normal life, because all that you have ever known is really abnormal.

So, we drink our lives away, smoke away our dreams and dare not to forgive our own relatives. Levels of disrespect are obvious and we justify our behavior by suggesting "only God can judge us," as if to say we can do whatever we want to do, period. These elements of survival become a place of retreat for us. Ultimately though, it runs the risk of being our suicidal refuge.

We speak to our own children in a very dysfunctional manner. They become your personal punching bag. You find fault with them as if they asked you to bring them here. We speak to them in tones that scar them for life, later wondering how they are where they are. "Stupid" becomes there nickname, as their first name is interchangeable with "Dumb," "Retarded" and "Just like your daddy, Jr." Parents blame their children for their own mistakes and constantly ignore the pain in shouting, "you are just like your daddy." This is hazardous because they sometimes hardly know or even respect their father. You make it difficult for your babies, as you give them your pain. The pain of being with a man you hoped to change. Now you subconsciously blame your children for your decisions. This is dysfunctional. Move forward and know he is still their father. Do not deny him the right to be present in their lives because you're caught up. Who he was as your man can be drastically different than his role as a father.

The pleasant place of sanctity is hard to achieve in the midst of dysfunction. As said earlier, your heart hurts because of the many painful realities you have endured and encountered in your life. You have thought of many things and perhaps suicide is one. Perhaps you have never contemplated truly taking your life, but you live your life as though it is already taken. Either way, you are living beneath the plan God has designed for you and what He desires of you. Unforgiving hearts, angry spirits and disruptive behavior are all elements of dysfunction. Few know that they are truly dysfunctional and willingly admit it as such. Besides it is easier to act as if we have it all together. Well, it is here that I again ask that you build a sanctuary of faith. How? First own your problem as your own problems. Second, with no excuses, atone with God.

As you own and atone, you take matters in your own hands to best create your personal sanctuary. You mature in your faith realizing that the school, church and family are all critical pillars of survival for our communities. You refuse to lose your right to function because of the abuse and dysfunctional realities around you. Your desire to live in greatness is paramount even when greatness is not within your family. You accept and realize that you are not destined for failure because your family fails you. The biggest thing to note here is that all families have levels of dysfunction. However, if we are not working together to be stronger, healthier and wiser, then we are killing our chances for greatness.

To this end, we can stop complaining about the peace we do not have in our communities until we win the war for our homes. The school, as an academic space of solace, and the church, as a spiritual place of peace, cannot replace your family. Our first order of business is to rebuild the broken elements of our families. We can no longer ask our children to be great when their idea of normal is defined by abnormal attitudes and behavior. The very function of our families have for too long been shaped by the obvious dysfunction.

If your sanctuary is in schools that disappoint you and a church that seems to judge you, not understanding you, then it is time to construct a non-suicidal sanctuary. When your mind begins to travel the decrepit tunnel of suicide because of your dysfunctional family, immediately arrest this thinking to the light of God that will carry you through a stronger tunnel of faith. As your heart tries to tell your body to bow down to pettiness and pitiful, handcuff such emotion and read your heart its rights of having to surrender to God.

Your personal sanctuary is your developed space of refuge. It is your right to live beyond what your circumstances try to say to you. It is your freedom to live and breathe and move at a pace that is peaceful. It is your liberty to better deal with your hurt heart. You have permission with your entire life ahead of you to instead kill the suicidal thoughts as a replacement for letting the suicidal thoughts kill you. Today you can build a private sanctuary of peace in your mind and love in your heart to save your soul. Remember you are a part of God's Royal Family and God is not a "baby daddy." He truly loves you. Trust Him. He created you to do great things. He will never leave you nor forsake you. Call on Him as the suicidal thoughts call on you. Know that you plus God equal an entire team of Champions. Don't just take my word for it, there's a greater Word than mine:

ROMANS 8:26-39
26 And the Holy Spirit helps us in our weakness. For example, we don't know what God wants us to pray for. But the Holy Spirit prays for us with groanings that cannot be expressed in words. **27** And the Father who knows all hearts knows what the Spirit is saying, for the Spirit pleads for us believers in harmony with God's own will. **28** And we know that God causes everything to work together for the good of those who love God and are called according to his purpose for them. **29** For God

knew his people in advance, and he chose them to become like his Son, so that his Son would be the firstborn among many brothers and sisters. **30** And having chosen them, he called them to come to him. And having called them, he gave them right standing with himself. And having given them right standing, he gave them his glory. **31** What shall we say about such wonderful things as these? If God is for us, who can ever be against us? **32** Since he did not spare even his own Son but gave him up for us all, won't he also give us everything else? **33** Who dares accuse us whom God has chosen for his own? No one—for God himself has given us right standing with himself. **34** Who then will condemn us? No one—for Christ Jesus died for us and was raised to life for us, and he is sitting in the place of honor at God's right hand, pleading for us. **35** Can anything ever separate us from Christ's love? Does it mean he no longer loves us if we have trouble or calamity, or are persecuted, or hungry, or destitute, or in danger, or threatened with death? **36** (As the Scriptures say, "For your sake we are killed every day; we are being slaughtered like sheep. **37** No, despite all these things, overwhelming victory is ours through Christ, who loved us.**38** And I am convinced that nothing can ever separate us from God's love. Neither death nor life, neither angels nor demons, neither our fears for today nor our worries about tomorrow—not even the powers of hell can separate us from God's love. **39** No power in the sky above or in the earth below—indeed, nothing in all creation will ever be able to separate us from the love of God that is revealed in Christ Jesus our Lord.

FIVE

[Black Parents ⏐ Black Family]

Photo courtesy of Jamel Shabazz

DID WILLIE LYNCH THE BLACK FAMILY?

I have a fool-proof method for controlling your black slaves. I guarantee everyone of you that if installed correctly it will control the slaves for at least 300 years. My method is simple, any member of your family or any overseer can use it.

I have outlined a number of differences among the slaves, and I take these differences and make them bigger. I use fear, distrust, and envy for control purposes. These methods have worked on my modest plantation in the West Indies, and it will work throughout the South. Take this simple little test of differences and think about them. On the top of my list is "Age," but it is there because it only starts with an "A"; the second is "Color" or shade; there is intelligence, size, sex, size of plantations, attitude of owners, whether the slaves live in the valley, on a hill, East, West, North, South, have fine or coarse hair, or is tall or short. Now that you have a list of differences, I shall give you an outline of action—but before that, I shall assure you that distrust is stronger than trust, and envy is stronger than adulation, respect, or admiration.

The Black Slave, after receiving this indoctrination, shall carry on and will become self refueling and self generating for hundreds of years, maybe thousands.

Don't forget, you must pitch the old Black vs. the young Black male, and the young Black male against the old Black male. You must use the dark skinned slaves vs. the light skinned slaves, and the light skinned slaves vs. the dark skinned slaves. You must use the female vs. the male, and the male vs. the female. You must also have your servants and overseers distrust all Blacks, but it is necessary that your slaves trust and depend on us. They must love, respect, and trust only us.

Gentlemen, these kits are your keys to control, use them. Have your wives and children use them. Never miss opportunity. My plan is guaranteed, and the good thing about this plan is that if used intensely for one year, the slaves themselves will remain perpetually distrustful.

The Willie Lynch Letter, supposedly written in 1712 by a slave master from the West Indies, provided a framework for the colony of Virginia on how to control its slaves. Although some have relied on this letter as "evidence" of today's problems with Black families, historians challenge the legitimacy of the letter. In various research-based circles, scholars have determined that the letter is inauthentic largely based upon the absence of a Willie Lynch during that time period. So, how does this conspiracy theory dominate our conversations as fact? Perhaps an answer is in the next question; did Willie Lynch the Black family?

In all the talk of the day on parenting and the Black family, surely we must acknowledge the auction block of slavery and its destructive effect in what we see today. Debatably, it was the auction block that served as the first official breakdown for our families on this side of the world. Sold away one-by-one, children, mothers and fathers were separated, many times never to see each other again. As slave fathers witnessed the lynching of their own bloodline, their manhood was compromised. As slave mothers were torn from their own children, yet asked to raise the slave master's children, their innate nurturing instincts were compromised. As slave children worked the plantation with no right to education, their innocence was compromised. While the slave master raped the slave woman away from the slave man, the Black family was ultimately compromised. Why all the conversation on the Black family as dysfunctional with little mention or reference to what fathered the dysfunction?

A pertinent discussion on the Willie Lynch Letter and its debatable authenticity is critical. Paramount to the conversation, however, is an anti-Black American history that best substantiates why many Blacks believe the letter. Sadly, many Black folk have been highly skeptical of America largely because of the evil that slavery produced. Willie Lynch, debatably a slave owner having lived in 1712, is sadly minimal to the fact that slavery as a function managed to disrupt, dismantle and destroy the Black family at its core.

The TV miniseries *Roots,* filmed in 1977, eloquently portrays this point in its riveting scene involving its central character, Kunta Kinte. Kunta, a slave from West Africa, was instructed to say his new name during a vicious whipping:

> Overseer: "Your name is Toby, I want to hear you say it. Your name is Toby, you're going to learn to say your name. What's your name?"

> Kunta: "Kunta, Kunta Kinte."

> Overseer: "When the master gives you something, you

take it. He gave you a name, it's a nice name, it's Toby, and it's going to be yours till the day you die. Now I know you understand me and I want to hear it...what's your name?"

With pride, Kunta, barely breathing, again repeats, "Kunta." Continually taking the lashes to his back while hanging by his wrists, fellow slaves plead for God's mercy on his behalf.

Overseer: "What's your name? Say it! Toby! Who are you? Say your name!"

Kunta: "Toby."

Overseer: "Say it again, say it louder so they all can hear you. What's your name?"

Kunta: "Toby, my name is Toby."

Overseer: "Aye, that's a good nigger. Cut him down."

This scene ends with Fiddler, played by Louis Gossett, Jr., emotionally tending to Kunta. In so doing he expresses:

"What you care what that White man call you...you know who you be! Kunta, that's who you always be, Kunta Kinte!"

Alex Haley's miniseries *Roots* profoundly captured an essential aspect of slavery, that of control. The control of the slave master was often used to invoke fear. This sometimes subjected the slave to such beatings as with Kunta or even death as a viable alternative. Perhaps the Willie Lynch Letter of 1712 is fabricated. Maybe Willie and his alleged letter are not responsible for lynching the Black family. One thing research has validated is the existence of slavery on America's shores in the year of 1712. It was slavery as we have learned that promoted a dysfunctional Black family, pitting Black folk against each other.

As witnessed in the scene described above, it's important to note that a Black man under the command of a White overseer whipped Kunta. It is equally important to note how Black women had no rights in raising their own children but were demeaned as wet nurses. Wet nurses were responsible for breastfeeding their slave masters' children. Again, maybe Willie is free from the indictment of lynching the Black family via this letter nearly 300 years ago. Conceivably, however, Willie Lynch's family, the slave masters of 1712, separated Black families on auction blocks, selling children away from their parents and parents away from each other. These sales of human beings produced maximum profit for the master's free labor as it also reproduced fear, self-hate and the very destruction we now label dysfunction.

Let us salute Alex Haley for his miniseries and book, *Roots*. While many critics have questioned the validity of *Roots*, Mr. Haley aided in bringing national attention to slavery and its functions. Whereas we acknowledge the historians for their work in disqualifying Willie Lynch as real, we honor history for exposing the ancestral family of Willie Lynch whom we hold responsible for its role in lynching the Black family.

BROKE AND BROKEN
— PARENTING

Yes, information is power. This is what many have often repeated as affirmation. Yet I believe it is the actualization of information received that is empowering. Who really wants to be empowered? I can share plenty of information with you, but if you choose not to actualize it in your life, then what good is any of it? Some of the most powerful informationis hidden in dusty books and shelved DVD's. Purchasing information on how to become rich will not innately mend your spending habits, nor will it eradicate the social forces that maintain who, in fact, gets rich in this country. Nevertheless, it is that very information that can supply you with necessary tools in curtailing your spending habits.

Black families have long endured the reality of being "broke." The premise of having only enough to just get by. In households throughout inner-city communities you can hear various complaints on how much we do not have. What was it about the families of yesterday that got by with little or nothing? How did they maintain family values and self-pride? This is not a story of the good ole' days, for it is those days, in critical assessment, which helped forge many of the challenges of these days. However, there is plenty to pay homage to regarding the families of a segregated past that maintained self-love and hope regardless of poverty.

In evaluation of our families, it is easy to detect a real challenge before us. Our parents, in many ways act like their children. Many cases can be made about why this is so. However, i must first acknowledge the many parents who despite their circumstances, choose to give their children the very best. All parents in urban communities are not pitiful, apathetic and absent. In fact, the opposite is true. There are many parents who give their all, putting their best food forward. Every daddy is not in jail or standing on street corners, and for those that are, there are just as many outstanding mothers who still desire what's best for their sons and daughters.

Positioned here are those parents who bring into the world what they do not raise in the world. The economic recession in my opinion did not create this problem. Newsflash! We have a history of not having much of America's wealth. In fact, we have a history of not having much monetarily. Being broke for many Black folks is not new, as many of us have grown up as such. This notion of being broke was often synonymous with having to forego one bill for another. For instance, the phone bill could wait considering the importance of the lights. Being broke is not unique to parents on public assistance only. Working families are broke and barely making it. Interestingly enough, Black folk today have more money, more access to economic opportunity, yet less to show for it.

I recall warm summer days where my parents would take us for "a ride." On these rides we would momentarily escape our neighborhood for the sake of seeing other parts of the city. My parents were very innovative. My dad, having grown up in Chicago's housing projects, would often take us through his childhood community. He was eager to show us this never changing environment, as he educated us on the power of choices. We would roll down State Street to the tune of my dad's lyrical wisdom, "these same guys were on the corners when I was younger and like them, those on the corners at home will be there when you get older."

These life lessons help me to write this essay. My parents worked very hard. My mom worked two full-time jobs. Inclusive of the money earned were the principles given. My parents often made me clear on how they "wanted for us what they did not have growing up." In my assessment, too many parents today have devalued the richness of teaching principle to their children. They have allowed their bank account to navigate their parenting. More hazardous are the parents that are obviously broken in their thinking as a part of broken families.

The notion of being broke is more than a notion. The assertion of being broken is catastrophic. They are not one in the same. Parents today come from broken environments. Their hearts are broken and too are their philosophies on life. Again, this is not new to Blacks and their families. The thinking has to be centered on how to create greater situations despite broken circumstances. First though we have to identify and own this as true. Twelve-step rehabilitation programs begin the first day you admit you have a problem. A compulsive drug addict cannot be admitted by the closest of relatives if he/she does not first admit they have the issue.

As such, we are in a crisis with our youth and it is time for negligent parenting to cease. As stated earlier, not all parents are broken nor are they broke. Broke parents do not have to condone brokenness. If you have little money, still encourage much morally. Television is not essential to your child's development, education is.

Demand more of your schools. Volunteer your time. Be the role model for the child in your neighborhood living without their dad or mom. Eliminate vulgarity from your vocabulary. It is lethal thinking to believe that your children will only do as you say and not as you do. What you do, more times than none they will model. You are the example. Act like it! Just because you have little in your pockets does not mean you have to act like you have little to show for life itself. Fix your home. Heal your heart. Seek counseling and predetermine that you will today break the curse of being absent. Remember broke ain't broken. Despite what money you do not have, take lessons from those before us; learn how to parent even on a fixed income.

In fact, fix your life and thus we shall see fixed communities. Then and only then can we see the value of, "if it ain't broke, don't fix it." Right now though as the older folk would say, "we got a whole lot of fixin' to do."

THE COSBY SHOW WAS
A DIFFERENT WORLD

One of the most exciting television moments for my generation happened to be the groundbreaking *Cosby Show,* followed by the sitcom *A Different World.* Every Thursday as 7:00 p.m. approached, regardless of what many of us were doing at the time, we all raced home for our one-hour hibernation. It is interesting to think about how much of an impact these two thirty-minute shows had on our lives and even our communities. What was it that most intrigued us as children? Why were we so willing to drop our playtime, even in summer months, to catch these shows on television?

The Cosby Show and *A Different World* were thirty-minute shows that depicted Black family in a very positive light. In hindsight, *The Cosby Show* is debatably responsible for some of the success in my generation. The show, which ran for nearly a decade, portrayed the Black family in a way unlike other stereotypical imagery of Blacks in media. Thus, it inspired hope and gave many of us a very tangible connection to successful Black Americans outside of what many of us lived.

As a married couple with five children, the Huxtable parents were professionals, with the father being a doctor and the mother an attorney. The show proved highly successful in that it was the only show to carry a #1 ranking for consecutive years. Despite its phenomenal television success, *The Cosby Show* took on a different and more powerful meaning for its Black viewers.

Adjoined to its eventual follow-up show, *A Different World* which highlighted young aspiring Blacks in college and on campus, these shows were socially relevant and informative. For many, it is safe to say that these stories were significant to a generation having mostly seen shows like that of *The Jeffersons, Good Times* and even *Diff'rent Strokes.*

Consider these sitcom themes: *The Jeffersons* was known for its classic display of a married couple, "movin' on up" and living atop a high-rise building with nominal wealth. The couple's neighbors and friends were an interracial couple who often fell victim to the main character, "George" and his signifying about their Black/White marriage; thus, *The Jeffersons* attempted to address various elements of race and culture.

Similar to this form of racial portrayal was *Diff'rent Strokes* where a wealthy White man, also living atop a high-rise building, adopts two Black children as his own. Many of these shows dealt with issues specific to daily life and growing up in a healthy household. Yet one cannot escape the obvious attempts made at showing racial solidarity on the television screen. The obvious point is found in the character of Mr. Drummond becoming an adopted father for the two young Black boys.

Most noteworthy here is *Good Times*, set in Chicago's housing projects, which told the all-too-familiar story of Blacks being poor and simply trying to make it. In many of their episodes, the Evans family of *Good Times* was caught in the vicious cycle of poverty. This family was caught in the wash of failed attempts to succeed due to discriminatory spins in their lives. They are ultimately unable to rinse themselves of the many obstacles that denied their progress, yet they band together as a family in phenomenal ways.

The Cosby Show differed from many shows in that it indirectly and widely attacked the negative imagery of Blacks in America. Moreover, unlike any show of our time, Cosby's challenged the myth of all Black families being unsuccessful, broke and broken. Typically, White families were seen as the organically loving people in households with stay-at-home mothers and nannies. The Cosby family challenged mainstream perspectives on who was deemed a healthy family racially.

Of grave significance is this connection between what was actually shown on television and what was literally lived every day. For example, as the country grappled with racial ignorance, discrimination and poverty, the television screen became an outlet to convey messages affirming these apparent problems within America's culture. For instance, James, the father in *Good Times,* was no less a man than Cliff Huxtable in the *Cosby Show.* He was no less a man than Cliff in *The Cosby Show.* James and his struggle to find work to care for his family connected strongly to the racism, oppression and inequality of his era. He, like Cliff, lovingly cared for each of his children and stood in the gap protecting his family as any man would; yet his desires were hampered by the economic and racial gaps that perpetually limited his options. Several episodes powerfully portray the effects of no jobs in the inner city and even limited educational attainment.

On the contrary, *The Cosby Show* was *A Different World* in that here existed a perspective television had long ignored; a world that kept *The Brady's* on the periphery of all of our lives. The wholesome, healthy family was always depicted through the lens of White people in America. Constantly, White men were the working breadwinners of the household as both parents sought to provide and protect their children. Quite possibly, the lyrics penned for the *Diff'rent Strokes* theme song fits this point well:

"A man is born, he's a man of means.

Then along come two, they got nothing but their jeans."

Mr. Drummond, having the "means," best provided for those two young Black boys (Arnold & Willis Jackson) as orphans from Harlem who had "nothing but their jeans." *The Cosby Show* receives two thumbs up in that it depicted in a very positive light a Black, married couple creating the means and buying the jeans. They worked successfully to obtain their "Little House on the Prairie" and this is the "Different World" we needed for television.

Most significant is *"A Different World"* needed for our families and communities today beyond television. From where I sit, *"The Cosby Show"* and *Good Times,* as different as their lives were, both offered a synergy of strength as family. Oddly, James and Florida, as parents living in the heart of Chicago's housing projects, managed to put food on the table with modest incomes from temporary (odd-in) jobs. One could easily argue that the greatest similarity between the Huxtable family and the Evans family was the maintained spirit of integrity as family.

What can we truly learn from these two shows? Well, despite what was not present in abundance and wealth, the Evans family persevered and stuck together. Likewise, despite an option to carry out an elitist attitude, the Huxtables were culturally connected. Both families maintained a spirit of integrity taking great pride in being a family. Florida, like Clair, both loved their husbands and best nurtured their households with levelheaded strength. JJ's artistic talent could easily afford him a scholarship that social elements did not seem to award him. Michael and Theo were both sons of phenomenal fathers who best exemplified strength, courage and wisdom. It is these attributes that surely nestled the daughters, Thelma, Sondra, Denise, Vanessa and Rudy.

What can we truly learn from these two shows specifically? Well, amongst so many things, Daddy Evans and Daddy Huxtable best demonstrated the power of being present. In being present they exemplified a spirit of perseverance. Each of the two persevered, despite any odds, as they provided for their families. They made no excuses as providers and we easily learn that their power was not because of money; Daddy Evans could attest to that. Their power was in their strength to love their family. Their power was connected to their desire to protect their household. This is the power our men of today must appreciate, ascertain and actualize; if "a picture is worth a thousand words," then your actual presence is priceless.

-SIX-

◇◇

[Black Fathers]

Photos courtesy of Dr. Chandra Gill

SHOOT THE BALL!

The message was made clear immediately after God plucked Daddy from the earthly garden of life, "grieve according to what you say you believe." As God spoke these words to me, I immediately altered my perspective on my daddy "dying" so abruptly and so tragically. At just the tender age of 59, on June 22, 2010, my daddy suffered a heart attack while at work. By the time I got to the hospital, then only knowing that he was admitted "unresponsive," my father was already gone, unbeknownst to me. In brief conversation with my brother as we awaited the nurse, I remember the feeling of wonderment and uneasiness. As we impatiently waited to see our daddy, a male nurse, who questioned our relationship to "Maurice Gill," finally greeted us. Shortly thereafter he asked that we follow him. As we walked toward the small room, I wondered if my brother knew what had been confirmed in my spirit; daddy was gone. As we listened to the nurse explain the details of daddy's arrival to the hospital and the "ten or so doctors" he said worked on him, I awaited the words that soon followed, "Maurice has passed."

No other moment best qualifies me to write this section, or this book for that matter. As a young girl, I learned early on the power in having my daddy present. Notwithstanding his physical stature, standing 6 feet 3 inches, it was his voice that intimidated many. Ringing as an entire bass section of a choir, when he spoke it resonated loudly. Perhaps this explains why just four days after my daddy's transition, so much of his message to me was loud and clear, "shoot the ball!"

As the confirmed commencement speaker for my high school alma mater's first class of 8th graders, I knew despite my loss, I had to speak as promised. As I pondered over how I would motivate graduates on one of their biggest days ever, I thought of my need for motivation in one of my most trying seasons ever. Interesting how God constantly subjected me to His power, however, as He reminded me that I was merely HIS vessel. If ever there came a time to confirm the strength of my relationship with God, surely, this was it.

Just four days after my daddy's transition, I entered the very building and hallways I for four years called home away from home. Once greeted by the assistant principal I was informed a rainstorm the night before had terminated the power to the auditorium where the ceremony was to occur. Moments later, I took my place in the processional of teaching staff and graduates. As we marched in, I looked around and thought of the many moments spent in this very gymnasium. How many games had I played in this very space? Now, exactly twenty years after my first practice and warm-up, there I sat, hearing my daddy's voice, "Shoot the ball!"

As the only girl on the basketball team in grammar school, I was the starting point guard. Despite this truth, I entered high school with no true desire to play anymore. After making the softball team, however, my teammates, in learning I could "shoot the ball," inquired of my interest in the basketball team for the coming fall. I accepted the opportunity my sophomore year, making the Varsity team for the starting forward position, and even playing the position of guard at times.

In each of my home games, my parents sat in the very bleachers that so many proud parents this day occupied with joy for their graduates. As I glanced around the gymnasium, I thought back to one of my first home games. Trailing our opponent, a timeout was called. At this moment, my dad yelled my name seeking my attention. With the attempt to huddle with my teammates and coach, he motioned for me to come near him, "Chandra, come here." Choosing my father over the team huddle, I briefly approached my dad at which time he ordered that I "shoot the ball." I vividly recall my dad sensing my hesitancy and the look on his face, and then his words, "Stop waiting on others to do what you already know how to do, shoot the ball." As I left his presence and went back to the team's huddle, I listened now to the coach's instruction, which did not quite parallel my daddy's order. With my coach moving me to the point guard position, perhaps it was my time to just "shoot the ball."

As I sat in this gymnasium two decades later, I suddenly remembered a scenario of my life that I had not thought of since my high school days perhaps. How amazing was God and my daddy as well in this throwback moment? As I brought the ball down court, I recall approaching the top of the key and shooting the ball. The shot rimmed in. I instantaneously looked over to my parents and my dad looked on seemingly unmoved as if to say, "I told you." His firmness was unmatched by any I have met in my lifetime so this moment was no different. After hitting my next three-pointer, I heard my daddy yell from the bleachers, "That's it, Chandra, keep shooting!" As I tried to recall whether or not we won that game, the meaning of it all began to unfold in my mind.

Here I sat as the keynote speaker for 8th grade students at my alma mater, hearing my dad's voice now speak to me via my own high school experience. "Shoot the ball" all of a sudden took on a very important meaning. Throughout my life, I have often tried to pass onto others that of what I was called to do. Admittedly, it took sometime for me to fully accept the gifts God had give unto me. Oftentimes, those around you, indirectly expect you to bow down to their insecurities. As you seek to respect the very nature of your relationships with those as family, friend, spouse, boss, pastor or teammate you lose the game in trying to keep others happy.

As a speaker, teacher, counselor, etc., I now see how I failed to use that moment on the court to translate into my life experiences off the court. I had in time failed to adhere to my daddy's wisdom and was still trying to pass the ball. The keynote message to me was candidly poignant, "Shoot the ball, Chandra!" No more apologizing for God's gifts on your life, "shoot the ball." Aim to not half step with your goals, play to win or ride the bench, and "shoot the ball." Look to play as a teammate, but don't expect others to do what you just might be best qualified to do, "shoot the ball." Stop before you pop (the ball), analyze the defense, incorporate your fellow teammates but be ready to, "shoot the ball." Near tears, I was suddenly very clear on my new relationship with my daddy and it came at a time where I could have passed the ball.

Just four days after my daddy left us, I wondered how I could deliver this speech. I constantly reminded myself of that last, long conversation with him where we too spoke about my busy speaking schedule for graduations this year. I knew that, inasmuch as I felt a bit nervous about this last graduation speech, there was simply no coincidence in it. I knew that this one was for Daddy. What I had not foreseen was how it was for my daddy in that he would speak to me, his daughter. I shot the ball, and kept my commitment as the speaker. I did not pass the ball for someone else to shoot. It is easy to assume that another speaker could have done the job just as well. The graduates are best equipped to measure what they feel they received on June 26th. Nevertheless, I know that I am best qualified to state that I profoundly positioned myself to hear my daddy and his lesson for me that day because I dared to take the shot. Had I passed it on to another colleague, surely the audience could have gotten what they needed, but I would have missed receiving what I needed to hear, "Shoot the ball!"

YOU ARE WHAT I AM
BUT COULD NOT BE

In my essay "Chains of Pain," I spoke of my daddy and granddaddy's pain within a society that rejected their presence, their very being. Interestingly, that chapter was constructed before my daddy unexpectedly made his transition. Months prior to his passing, several e-mail exchanges took place. In one e-mail response regarding his return to school for his collegiate degree, I told my brother that our parents provided the way for us to be who and what we are. I cc'd our parents in that reply and my daddy's response was:

> "You are what I am but could not be. I am whom I am yet I thrive to be more. Faith and Love are intertwined in relationships and they can be separate, I prefer the latter. Chandra and Marcus, love of family is forever you will be what is destined and our children will attain what we continue to seek. All Praises To Our Lord for giving us life. LOL Dad."

"You are what I am but could not be," is a stark reminder and reflection of daddy's love, passion and intellect. Masterfully written and conveyed are the words that we now have as mere memories. I am all of what he is as his daughter yet that of what I also am is what he was unable to be. As his daughter, I am grateful for his presence, his power and his profundity. What happens when young men and women are not aware of who their parents are? My dad placed strong emphasis on giving us, his children, much more than what he received in his childhood. What happens when young men and women are not provided for and protected?

There are many that can attest to the power of having great parents. Clearly, not all parents abandon their children. In fact, many parents work extremely hard to ensure a better future for their children. Such parents take their responsibilities seriously fully understanding their roles. In contrast, however, striking imbalances often exist in the lives of those suffering from parental abandonment. As conversations continue to grow regarding the importance of young men having their fathers present, there is also a strong need for dialogue concerning young ladies and their fathers.

Fathers are just as critical and pivotal to their child's development as are mothers. Often we here the proverb, "It takes a village to raise a child"; well, who's the village? Too often this "village" is a replacement for the roles of parents. The "village" has had to step in and do for children what parents sometimes opted out of. While there is plenty of conversation being tossed around concerning parental involvement, I deem it necessary to mention the role of my daddy in my life.

I now understand, that many young women fail in their relationships due to their father's absence. Having my daddy around was more than his reprimands for me to clean my room and getting good grades. His presence provided me with a sense of protection and covering. The more I think of my dad's jewels of wisdom, the more I realize why material jewelry from men never impressed me. I have often said to men I date that my daddy helped me become the woman I am today. In that, I let brothers know that a movie and dinner were not the precursor to my goods as their dessert.

Admittedly, many women today have been abused physically, leading to their promiscuity and extreme sexual behavior. On the other hand, some women have been abused emotionally as they suffer from a form of abuse that we must start to label as such, *absenteeism*. When daddy is absent in a young girl's life, depending on the nature of such, subconscious scars develop. The void is thus created leaving young girls vulnerable in this oftentimes, cruel world.

Too often we have only considered fathers violent in households where physical abuse is present. We fall short on other areas of violence sometimes connected to alcoholism, drug addiction or repeat behavior from their own childhoods. In that vein, is not absenteeism somewhat violent and abusive? When fathers abandon their children, the violent act is emotionally and psychologically taxing on children. Young women, in particular, go through life looking for their boyfriend to be what they did not have in their father. This is a subconscious behavior for many as it is common to ignore why we do what we do. Many of our young men, having not their father growing up, are angry, hurt and displaced emotionally. Their pain is connected with subconscious realities that they are unable to identify. These young girls and boys soon become parents themselves, often resulting in the very behaviors that proved destructive to their own potential.

While there are various exceptions, overwhelmingly, children without parents in general and daddy in particular, undergo tremendous pain and setback. When unresolved, their established behaviors are passed down to newer generations. Many adults have become volatile, angry and unproductively scarred adults because of absentee parents. The words of my daddy, "you are what I am but could not be," then takes on a new meaning; adults soon become all of what their parents are.

The presence of a great father is paramount in the life of both boys and girls alike. I speak as a daughter recognizing all of what my father meant to me. As he spoke to me personally, "you are what I am but could not be," I imagined he realized the fruit of his labor. Many obstacles stood in the way of his comprehensive success as a young Black man, yet nothing prevented him from being a successful father. The message is quite simple; we need fathers who shall let nothing stand in the way of raising their children. If parenting is an option for brothers, then my daddy's words are reverse resulting in this constant generational curse. Children will thus become only that of what their father is, in absence, and never what they could be in fullness.

IF GOD IS NOT A "BABY DADDY," THEN...

Fannie Lou Hamer, an activist fighting for the voting rights of Black folk during the Civil Rights struggle stood with great courage. Having been beaten by White police officers and jailed in her efforts, she was left partially disabled for the remainder of her life. Nonetheless, Sister Hamer's courage led her to the organization of the Mississippi Freedom Democratic Party (MFDP). In 1964, the MFDP asked the National Democratic Party to seat their chosen delegates in the all-White upcoming National Democratic Convention. After being denied such, they were allowed to make a presentation concerning their needs and wants.

As the chosen spokesperson, August 22, 1964, Sister Hamer provided a moving account of the violence she and so many other Blacks had endured in trying to gain a right to vote in Mississippi:

> "Is this America, the land of the free and the home of the brave, where we have to sleep with our telephones off the hooks because our lives be threatened daily, because we want to live as decent human beings in America?"

Fannie Lou Hamer having only received up to six years of formal education stood in the face of Senators and other Democratic leaders with conviction. She was soon offered two non-voting seats at the convention at which she refused to accept. Having a focus beyond the acceptance of crumbs and compromises, Sister Hamer later exclaimed,

"All my life I've been sick and tired. Now I'm sick and tired
of being sick and tired."

How many of us are "sick and tired" of "baby mama drama" and "baby daddy" talk? As Sister Hamer demanded that of what was fair, right and just she settled for nothing less. Moreover, she challenged a system that insisted she remain silent. Despite her limited formal education, she is quoted as one who loved to read and known as a great speaker. With religious convictions, Sister Hamer's spirit is perhaps what many in our communities need today.

As we continue to battle for human rights, on the rise are issues within our communities that we can rectify without petitioning politicians in the political process. Simply put, we do not need a majority vote to tear down the walls of ignorance. "Baby daddy" conversation sounds too much like an acceptance of absent fathers. Interestingly enough, this leads me to a conversation on our Royal Father. Can you imagine God being our "baby daddy?" God, in all of His love for us, grants us favor as He constantly provides for us. Even in our most downtrodden and rebellious state, God remains our Father, hearing our prayers and answering our calls. Can you imagine our Royal Daddy being a "baby daddy?" As One who cares for us, provides for us, protects us and yet teaches us, He never fails us.

Quite frankly, "I am sick and tired of being sick and tired" as well. The way in which we treat one another is simply unacceptable. Our communities have suffered far too long because of our lack of obedience. We casually accept too much foolishness. Is God our step-father? Is he a mere "baby daddy?" I stand as Sister Hamer with conviction and courage proclaiming that, if God is not a "baby daddy" then surely we need not accept others choosing foolishness over family.

This is a message to men who settle for being the "baby daddy" and not a replica of our Royal Father. For women, whom laughingly excuse men of their responsibilities, refusing to challenge them beyond sex, this is for you. This is a memo to parents who no longer have a working relationship with one another, thus holding the children in a haven of "baby mama drama" and "baby daddy" lingo.

The Voting Rights Act of 1965 was largely realized because there were those who were just "sick and tired of being sick and tired." They stood in honor of their Royal Father as they fought against ignorance and evil. As our Royal Father, God honored such courage, conviction and community. It is time we best understand that very power we represent. God is not a "baby daddy." Sure, God is affectionately our daddy. And yes, our fathers are affectionately called daddy; but the reality of what a "baby daddy" has produced by and large must cease. It is not cool for brothers to reject their responsibility. This marathon away from responsibility will run laps of failure around your children's future. Stop running away from your child's life and their needs! Irrespective of the circumstances and lack of finances, the time is now to mature, grow and set aside childish ways so that you can best father your children. If not, you are solely passing the baton of failure to your "seeds." Their chances of victory are then distorted all because of your inability to produce favorable results for their future.

While we can call God our daddy, many of us must stop acting like babies. Our attitudes toward are children must be to properly train them, spiritually mold them and lovingly care for them. God is not a "baby daddy." As His children, made in His image, we must grow beyond the "baby daddy" syndrome. Are you yet "sick and tired of being sick and tired"? If so, then treat children as high valued "seeds" and try planting them in fertile ground. Make every attempt to provide them the most organic experiences as they grow. In so doing, God will harvest in your life the beautiful fruit of your labor.

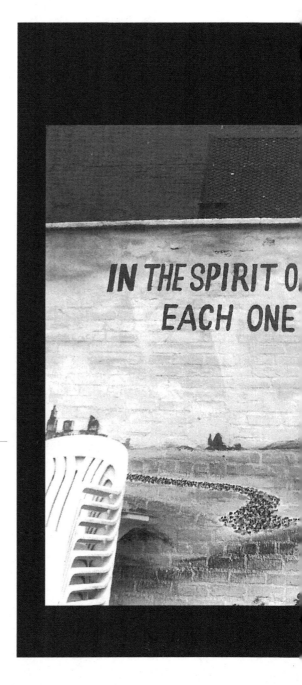

SEVEN

THE MILLION MAN MARCH
JUST REACH ONE!

Photo courtesy of Jamel Shabazz

DREAM KEEPERS AND DREAM KILLERS

In writing this essay, I have been intellectually assigned to challenge you in the area of dreaming. I believe quite candidly that sleepers dream. While asking a child to dream is important, I believe just as significant is creating a world where dreams become realities. Many of us are familiar with a few very popular dreams:

> There is the dream where you are asleep and, while asleep, you dream of falling from a cliff, the edge of your bed or some high space. Before you hit the bottom, you are awakened.

> There is the dream where you seemingly fight spirits. As you asleep, your entire body is arrested. You fight trying to wake up.

> Then there are those dreams that you forget yet remember. It is strange to remember and forget, all at once. While you feel that the dream is necessary to remember, you just can't recall any of the details.

Instead of taking my inexperienced route of a psychologist, I yield some incredible truths unto you sociologically.

First, to dream outside of sleep is to do what is called daydreaming and often synonymous to "staring into space." Daydreaming, is interesting because wherever you might be at that time, you are taken away from that moment, that assignment, etc., to think about something that happened or to fantasize about something you want. One important thing to highlight here is that the outsider cannot tell the difference of one daydreaming and "staring into space." Many would argue that the daydreamer isn't just "staring in space." Perhaps they are fantasizing in some way or envisioning an ideal moment. However one chooses to view the difference, is okay. For me, it is just imperative for us to have the conversation regarding what it means to dream. For those that are asleep, dreams produce significant revelation and even confirmation. It is in dreams that many see things that they truthfully had not dreamed of seeing before, no pun intended. Many prophets dreamed and thus later prophesied. Such dreams keep many experts unable to truly account for said power(s).

It is critical to place this context and groundwork with dreaming in its proper perspective. In short, and specific to my point, literal dreams often happen in one's sleep. For many within urban communities, this is actually hazardous as the operative word here is sleep. If we really want our youth to dream the unthinkable, as the mantra goes, (which I challenge) then we have to awake them into a consciousness. Far too many of us, generally speaking, are sleepwalking zombies. Such realities inevitably produce a limited thinking and being in life. Institutions such as schools and churches speak volume to dreaming without this context. Further, too much emphasis is placed on dreaming to achieving while the dreamer is socially, spiritually and psychologically strangled daily. It is like having someone with his or her foot on your neck while you are face down on the ground, telling you to get up. In your mind, you are more than willing to at least try if they would just remove their foot. Our children spend their lives subconsciously fighting to remove the feet of oppression, racism, discrimination and low expectations, still struggling to just stand up.

Dream Keepers are individuals and institutions that condone success beyond the dream. Besides, how productive is a dream you cannot recall? How advantageous are dreams, if they fail to speaks to one's reality? Dreams in and of themselves are not good enough in dealing with unchallenged power structures.

Dream Killers are teachers, police officers, friends, family, doctors, lawyers, employers, employees, White, Black, Asian, Latino, etc., that suppress any forms of dreams for anyone. They are CEO's, entertainers, pastors and priests. They are the counselors that discourage youth from applying to schools based on what they can't see for a child's future. Dream killers are parents that provide no vision nor hope for their child(ren) based on their own limited success. They discourage growth in their children by abusing the process for their child's success. Dream Killers are politicians afraid to pass legislation that will level the playing field and allow all children opportunity. They insists on maintaining ideology that pad the next two, three, or more years for their political career. They refuse to change and challenge laws that can legally destroy the chains of inequity and inequality.

Dream Killers aid in the destruction of our children's lives. Dream Keepers aid in the development of our children's minds.

CHRISTOPHER COLUMBUS DISCOVERED JESUS— THAT'S MY FINAL ANSWER

As children, many of us learn the importance of telling the truth. Honesty was indeed "the best policy" for so many reasons. Who wanted to associate with a liar? I recall, in my elementary school days, a young man would often tell lies. Sadly, when his name was mentioned, no one warmly received him because of his dishonesty.

Likewise, for years I learned that Christopher Columbus discovered America. Admittedly, it was rather disengaging having to sit in history class with these untruths. Still today, I question my school's curriculum. How did he receive so much credit for just running into people on accident? The bigger question is how could those very same history books isolate the truth of Blacks and their contributions from not only this country but also the entire world? Why was the truth of our ancestors and their inventions camouflaged beneath such myths as Columbus and his charade of discovery?

Whereas some have minimized these magnified lies, I believe there are many damaging effects that can result from such false material. Earlier, I mentioned how urban youth perpetually devalue more of themselves through their own behavior. Yet, this devaluing starts within a societal framework, which insists on them being inferior. Again, if all that you learn of yourself is criminal, dirty and degrading then your challenge in life is the uphill climb of proving you are not those things. Many, however, succumb and accept this as real. They act criminal. How could they not? Everything that is good looks unlike them and all that is ugly is every bit of them. The most powerful thing attributed to "the White man" was his kidnapping of Jesus and America.

Think about it this way: Jesus, as our Lord and personal Savior is for many in America a "White man." To question his race for far too many is blasphemous. Interestingly enough, this same line of thinking is tolerated in the arguments regarding Christopher Columbus. It's the argument of "it matters not." Well, it does matter! To conveniently hijack discovery and debatably salvation is what is blasphemous, not the questions and research to suggest otherwise. Black children have been trained to some degree from early stages to hate the very essence of who they are because of such foolishness. Schools and other institutions should be held accountable for such as it is destructive on so many levels to encourage immoral behavior, especially lies in the two most valued institutions in Black communities. What happens when people lie in of all places, the church and school, where you are to get education and edification? Will somebody please tell mama?

The "White man" is all in Your Mind

So who is this "White man" anyway? To what do we accredit his existence as oh-so-powerful? Slavery, as an institution, was incredibly powerful in its dehumanization for all those involved, not just those enslaved. It was responsible for giving a false sense of power to the slave-owners while simultaneously giving a false sense of powerlessness to those forced to live as slaves. Being enslaved in America perpetually empowered the demon of racism. The sense of power that I reference here is widely adjoined to what it means to belong to God, the All-powerful. Did God create one race of people as greater than another? Why relegate darker skin to statuses and even statues of powerlessness? Such imposed ideologies, I argue, falsely empowered those not necessarily stronger or more intelligent but spuriously privileged. In other words to reduce Africans and their genius to mere slaves with laws that substantially supported their inferiority created generations of mental bondage that shrewdly discredited their lineage. It's like telling Jews that Jesus wasn't their kind, or was He?

The history of White men as powerful in this country is connected to privileges granted centuries ago. Many of today's companies and corporations have long histories. I sometimes find myself in certain stores that say they have been established since the 1850s or '60s, and I think to myself, wow, my people couldn't own themselves then, let alone stores. Laws that prevented Blacks from being fully human made them property to be bought and sold. They were owned by White men who perpetually empowered their own ideologies of Blacks being worth nothing more than slaves for them. The hateful and horrifying acts committed at that time were nothing short of sinful. The disdain the slaves felt in those years was associated with their institutional subjugation. The very White men that owned them owned the laws and owned their families. Moreover, White men acquired and ultimately owned money, and lots of it. Slaves were overworked and hardly paid. Their pay overwhelmingly came by way of scraps called food and clothes. The distribution of wealth was solely generational as was the poverty Blacks would overwhelmingly pass down generation to generation.

The discourse on the "White man" is rooted in complexities touched on here. It is Important to mention, all White men are not evil. Just as important, however, are those privileges associated with being White in America. Whiteness in America has been generationally problematic. A quick assessment on how beauty is defined in America helps us to see this. Videos, commercials and other media outlets, depicts a portrait of beauty in total opposition to other ethnic groups and their genetic make-up, particularly Blacks. Long, straight hair for instance consumes many Black women, as much as our desires to be slim. f course, this isn't solely a Black pandemic. However, considering the perpetual damaging effects and history of Blacks as property, there is a deep question to be asked here which is: how could a group so oppressed in society dare and strongly desire to look as their oppressor? Said another way, the question becomes, how and why are Black folk so consumed with hating their Blackness and wanting to exchange it for what they were neither born to become nor can ever be?

As highlighted constantly in these essays via the lens of Chains, the mental enslavement and bondage of a people communicates and translates into unhealthy messages, leading to shameful attitudes and behavior. The thinking is poisonous and thoughtless. The "White man" thus becomes one who is all in your mind literally and figuratively.

In slavery, Blacks were forced to succumb involuntarily to powers largely physically, while debatably many Blacks today succumb voluntarily to such power mentally and institutionally.

The point is then made that the "White man" is not some White man roaming the earth seeking to destroy all Black men. The ideology of an existent "White man" is connected to a history of White men and what they have done historically in America. White men have enjoyed privileges in this country per their own establishment. White people thus benefit from these same privileges because they empowered themselves while disempowering Blacks and others. This is an important fact to mention. Just because I enslave you does not mean I am better than you. It does not mean I am greater than you. It does not mean I am stronger, more intelligent nor wiser. In fact, it can mean the exact opposite.

My point is that the "White man" phenomenon is couched in a real history. It is important to realize that this "White man" is ideologically attached to White supremacy in America. It is institutional and thus mental. It is greater than the "White man" as man; it is "White man" as mind. To understand this in totality is to analyze why it is you think what it is you think about daily? If you desire to be great because it's the White thing to do, then you are a victim. If you desire to be smart because many White people are smart, then you are a victim. If you feel Blacks are dumb, yes, you too are a victim, and if you feel as a White person that you deserve greatness because of your color and not God, then victim you are too!

From where I sit, this is one of the largest challenges of America today. Our infatuation as American citizens further polarizes the race problem here in America. It is sensationalized, extremely detrimental and at best, propaganda. The Black-White test score gap is an example of such. Researchers and practitioners suggest constantly that Black students under-perform their White counterparts on standardized tests. Black students are challenged in the area of not performing well. The mindset itself is skewed on this matter for varying reasons.

First, to constantly measure the success of Black students through the lens of White students is illegitimate ideology. Why? In so doing, we make White students the standard. White students as a whole are no more the standard than the successful African students that outscore them on tests. Students from other countries tend to test better than America's students; therein is the challenge for America. Why are America's students outperformed globally? Why are we not competitive with China, India and other developed countries? I hear little mention of an American-Chinese test score gap that insists White students are lazy or unintelligent. Better still, how about we raise the issue of a White-Asian test score gap or an African-White test score gap. Those who travel here in search for education prove to work hard and dominate fields such as the sciences, technology, medicine, etc.

Overall, the Whiteness epidemic in America is not some made-up lie. It is the Whiteness of America that perpetually defines White as great and all other ethnicities as "the other." This Whiteness has a history of conquering for the sake of greed. This Whiteness is not a "White man" per se, for it can also be Black cops that hate their own, Latino judges that uphold racist policies, Black teachers that don't like their Black students and even Black ministers that uphold a White Jesus while insisting that color does not matter. Issues relevant to race in America helps produce the demon of racism. We cannot afford to ignore the obvious. Racism is as real to oppressed groups, as the white man is to America's history.

-EIGHT-
◇✕◇

[Black Talk | Communication]

Photo courtesy of Jamel Shabazz

IF YOU LIKE IT, I LOVE IT!

For too long, old sayings in our community have been passed down and repeated without question; "If you like it, I love it." "Anything in moderation is okay." "We all have to die from something." These age-old quotes have, unfortunately, survived too many generations and far too many of us accept them as a philosophy for our lives. If language has cultural power, then we must reevaluate these sayings. We must dare to ask if any of them are out of step with where we should be today or if they represent irresponsible ways of thinking and being.

Consistent with my childhood years, I recall various games we played in my neighborhood. "Simon Says" and "Follow the Leader" were played and they suggested being in tune with the chosen or even self-appointed leader. At the leader's command you were to do as instructed in both games. For some reason, neither game really worked for me. As the leader in both games, it was admittedly pretty exciting telling others what to do and how to do it. However, I was easily bored as these games were engaging only for a short period of time.

Admittedly, "Follow the Leader" was somewhat more versatile than "Simon Says." "Follow the Leader" was just that. Whatever the leader said is what one would do, no questions asked. Irrespective of how many followers played, the leader was one who instructed all on what movements to make and even what could be said. If he/she instructed silence, then that was the rule until talking was permitted. If the leader commanded yelling with the right hand up, all would then yell until the leader stopped or transitioned to the next bodily or verbal movement.

"Simon Says" was also centered on leaders and followers, though it was a bit more robotic. "Stop," "go," and "freeze" were the common words. At the command of Simon the leader, you were to do as instructed. The objective with this game was clearer here. One could actually win, although that was seldom the case in my neighborhood. The goal was to have all participants in line, side by side and several feet away from Simon. Simon would simply stand in the same position several feet from the other participants while commanding how they should move. With each robotic step, the participants were to listen carefully to Simon and move accordingly. The objective was for the participant to get to Simon with keen listening and an ability to take commands. This was sometimes very tricky.

Simon, having all power, could command, "go, go, go, go, go" and then "stop" only for several participants to find themselves unable to suddenly stop, thus Simon says "you're out." It was then that you had to go back to the beginning and start all over. Depending upon Simon's mood, the game could go on forever. For me, in fact, the game was actually one big trick centered on Simon never giving up his/her leadership. Thus, he/she would muster up ways to facilitate losing as opposed to there ever being a winner. In other words, getting to and replacing Simon as the leader was virtually impossible, as they would almost always deny someone taking their place.

"Dirty Snatch," "Cobs" and "Left/Right Hand, Give it up" were more of my childhood games. Dirty Snatch was simple. No matter the day or time, once a participant, always a participant. Simply, if I desired something you had, by virtue of me wanting it and calling out "Dirty Snatch," I could take that which was yours.

"Cobs" was a game that entailed saying "cobs" in order to position oneself to share in what was purchased or brought to the table by another. The way out of this game was to always find yourself suggesting "no cobs." This game proved to be quite hilarious, as you would literally find yourself at the register paying for your food items and immediately screaming "no cobs" as you pay the cashier. In so doing, you were now freed from having to share.

"Left/Right Hand, Give it up" was interesting in that you were to give up all things in your left or right hand (the hand was determined by the group playing). If playing and carrying your lunch in your left hand, another could say "left hand give it up" and you were no longer owner of your own lunch, thus giving it up. These three games were all very common to the children of my neighborhood and were played during school lunch periods, recess or while outside in parks.

During my childhood years, these games and sayings offered much excitement and probably mentally conditioned us as well. As with any child, whether rich or poor, our curiosity and zeal for life was subjected to our surroundings. Specific to my inner city childhood years, levels of enjoyment were invented on street corners due to a severe absence of resource centers and other productive outlets. Arguably, the creative genius of children in the inner city is shown when having to make something out of nothing because of what was not offered in our communities.

Children of today have more at their disposal considering the technological advancements of our time. It is pleasing to hope for those days of yesterday. To be quite honest, even those days had great challenges. In fact, those days have been glorified and not truly analyzed. People who lived during that era have often failed to tell the stories. It has always been vital for generations to hammer out the challenges of the world fearlessly and faithfully. The youth of today did not create these problems alone.

Individual responsibility is one of our greatest cures. When it is all said and done, we must prove accountable for our own behavior, irrespective of who momma is and even who daddy might not be. It is no easy pill to swallow. I have learned often that "the enemy is the inner me." Wisdom teaches us to take responsibility. In fact, it is here where we attack that saying, "experience is the best teacher." I know that God's wisdom is our best teacher. From where I sit, experiences can hurt you but wisdom helps guide you. It is wisdom, if adhered to, which can keep you from unnecessary experiences. Sure, experiences help shape you, but they are not the "best teacher."

When we respect God's wisdom as our "best teacher" and guide, we are then positioned to cure ourselves and solve our own problems! We can hear what He has to say on the matters of our communities and even the language we use culturally. As for me, no, I do not like it just because you love it. This is foolishness. I, in fact, love you too much to support your liking what is potentially damaging to you. No, any and everything in moderation is not good for us. Crack-cocaine is never good for you. Certain things are intolerable and, yes, we will all die from something, yet this does not mean that we have to alter God's life span for us by choosing to die early. These conflicting messages must go!

We must get to a place where we choose to be champions in what we speak. We must get involved and take action against damaging thoughts and words! Today, let us take action in our lives, screaming "no cobs" on our faith while "dirty snatching" all that is necessary for our development. "Left hand," give up fearful words and sinful behavior. "Right hand," give up language couched in bitterness, pain and troubles of yesterday. Call "cobs" on millionaire mentality over purchased poverty. Follow the leadership of God and His wisdom. He is flawless. He created you with tender-loving care. In so doing, He has a plan for you. Regardless of what you have not gotten in your life thus far, choose to challenge what is said around you and change what comes out of you. Words are powerful. Examine your speech today and "dirty snatch" language that is something to like and more for your children to love.

IF 'IF' WAS A FIFTH, WE'D ALL BE DRUNK

But Moses protested again, "What if they won't believe me or listen to me? What if they say, 'The Lord never appeared to you'?" Exodus 4:1

Called to lead the children of Israel from bondage, Moses carried on his back arguably one of the greatest tasks of all time. How could he, a mere murderer, a man abandoned and left by a riverbank as a child, hear from God for such a mandate? As a little Hebrew boy subjected to laws ordering his death upon birth, he seemingly never had a real chance for a productive life. On many accounts he was, in fact, doomed for failure considering a society legally opposed to him living let alone winning. When he questioned God regarding the children of Israel and their potential responses to him as their savior, clearly his questions were justified.

In the spirit of Black talk within our communities, we introduce some and remind many others of a saying that is perhaps very familiar, "If 'if' was a fifth, we'd all be drunk." This famous saying was a rebuttal often given when someone would utter the word "if." Some would assert what they would do "if" they possessed something else to get it done. Others would remark what could be done "if" time or resources permitted. Nonetheless, the sharp comeback, "If 'if' was a fifth, we'd all be drunk," made us clear on just how much weight had been given to the usage of the word itself. Clearly, the fifth pint of liquor could intoxicate many and "if" this word were to appear as that bottle of liquor, we would all "be drunk." Subsequently, what we have then is what I conclude as an intoxication of the word "if" itself. The obvious overuse of the word is what produces this catchy and poignant phrase. Imagine being asked by God to go on a mission for Him and your responses are all based on what you think might happen. Moses, perhaps in some shock over God's request, leaned more on his insecurities and lack. He was trapped in what we will call the "what/if" syndrome. I ask now, what if "if" really were a fifth?

Are you like Moses in that you have been tapped by God to move ahead, yet you are trapped in your own doubts that hold you back? Instead of hearing more that God has to say on the matter for your calling, you interrupt his conversation with the fear of what might happen. You cut God off in His conversation to you just to make the point of how you might not be received or what others might think. Your calling in life is thus connected to conditions you have shaped in your mind as real; it is the "what/if" syndrome.

Like Moses, many of us deal in the arena of wonderment with God. We have produced a circus of dreams therein and refuse to choose an ambitious faith. "What if" the seats of your stadium were limited to high faith-based paying fans? "What if" drinking was prohibited in this arena, best preventing any intoxication on the word "if"? "What if" you officially introduced abstinence to the "what/if" syndrome, thus kindly welcoming a thirty-day trial of discipline opposing "if" and its cousin "what if"?

Perhaps many of you are trapped in this arena of wonderment with God. Are you shocked and amazed at what He has put forth for you to do? You also wonder why He would select you to do such great work. Clearly, Moses was just this little Hebrew boy who happened to be simply tending to his father-in-law's flock. His life's chances were limiting on many accounts. Yet, there are some intriguing components to this man Moses that may elevate you.

Moses was left at the riverbank because his mother could no longer hide him. This mandate at the time to kill all Hebrew boys was a serious matter and she had done all she could to conceal him. After three months, she left him at the Nile River, generally regarded as the longest river in the world. While it is relatively easy to see the dangers presented to Moses at birth, having a death wish on his life from the beginning, it is also attractive to give credence to the protection and covering he received.

There he laid, a newborn alongside the river soon to experience the longevity of God's covering and mercy. Having not a chance by legal standards, this Hebrew boy stole the heart of one at the riverbank. She happened to be a princess and her father was the king responsible for issuing the mandate against all Hebrew boys. According to scripture, Moses' sister, desiring to see what would happen to her brother, stood at a distance until he was found. It was her interaction with the princess that brought Moses back home to be nursed and nurtured. Having then experiencing the length of God's grace at the riverbank, Moses encountered the breadth of God's existence as a newborn.

Since childhood, some of us have heard "what" we could do "if" we had this or "if" we had that. Some of us were challenged by great parents to leave "if" at the door as "when" walked in; well, it is now that we revisit and clean up our speech. God is not a God of "if," He is a God of "when." In other words, "when" He calls, He expects us to respond, at worst, with "when." His words on and for our lives are not couched in conditions of what may or may not happen. He has already promised us and His promises are greater than gold. He does not expect us to take on any mission only for us to lose and fail. In God is the victory that shall be performed through us.

"If" you have been met by wonderment, amazed at the ideas you have and the pull to get it done, then the time is now to seek and see. Here you sit at the riverbank, a newborn in your faith having already encountered the length of God's blessings and unable to see yourself beyond your fears. Watching to see what will happen and how you will respond are angels waiting to talk on your behalf. Needing to do nothing other than be available to start, God sends one closest to your opposition to act on your behalf, seeing to it that you are nursed and nurtured. It is then paramount for us to not wonder about what will happen. This blueprint should deactivate responses including "if" with God. Besides, as it is written, "No eye has seen, no ear has heard, no mind has conceived what God has prepared for those who love him." (1Corinthians 2:9) So "if" you love God, you are invited to a healthy intoxication of God's word and, thus, His blessings; "No "if," "ands," or "buts" about it!"

CONVICTION:
IT'S A WHOLE 'NOTHER LEVEL

How does a country as powerful and wealthy as the U.S. parade a one in seven statistic when it comes to its poverty rate? How is it possible that America, the 'land of the free,' incarcerates more of its citizens than any other country in the world? These realities are alarming and sadly indicative of our condition as a country in this new century. Deplorably, these realities exasperate the author concerning the African-American communities. As America lags the world in educational achievement and success, this says profoundly that those lagging in America are further behind the world's populace. From a personal standpoint, as stated earlier, this expands the conversation on what the achievement gap really is, taking it to a whole 'nother level.

A whole 'nother level is, oddly enough, a form of discourse found in conversational circles across race and class lines. Various professionals, even newscasters, are heard emphasizing their positions by saying, "That's a whole 'nother level." In several of my lectures on this topic, I have found it interesting that so few actually question the grammatical positioning of such as they genuinely use it themselves. Laughingly, many had not even considered just how incorrect this terminology is. Simply put, it is affectionately used as a point of reference when strongly emphasizing one's position or thought. In that, I am led to discuss what truly is "a whole 'nother level."

One in 100 citizens in the United States of America are incarcerated. What do we make of this astounding statistic and how do we account for this? All the more painful are the convictions of so many of our youth. Here we will not toss around the all too familiar statistics surrounding the prisons as a multi-billion dollar business. This is all-too-familiar territory, albeit very necessary to review in deciding how we can begin to see and understand the magnitude of it as a problem. The conviction of Black folk in America's judicial system is a whole 'nother level. The policies outwardly aimed at their convictions in court are outright disrespectful. To that end, it is imperative that we turn this thing around.

On one hand, conviction is, by definition, an unwavering belief in something without need for proof or evidence. On the other hand, it is a final judgment of guilty in court cases and the punishment that is imposed. I seek to take the conversations on convictions of our youth and those marginalized in targeted communities to a whole 'nother level. See, it is quite easy to sit idly by, discussing the magnitude of the legal system as problematic. Have we best understood, though, that when people are unfairly convicted in courtrooms and sentenced to decades for crimes they have not committed, this harms their families and our communities all the more? Do we realize that many judges, more than what we care to believe, make decisions on a whole 'nother level themselves as they wrongfully and arrogantly interpret cases in the name of constitutional law? We have judges that wrongfully use conviction (and its various definitions) as they lean on their "unwavering belief," thus wrongfully convicting Black folk "without need for proof or evidence."

The all-too-familiar convictions from judges in courtrooms have led to unfair sentencing, which at times, resulted in capital punishment. Is it not evil to take someone's life at the mercy of a wrongful conviction? Over and over again we are hearing of stories where brothers and sisters are exonerated only after spending decades in jails for crimes they did not commit. These bogus convictions are sadly downplayed as, one by one, innocent brothers and sisters are now being released from jails. Do we not get the point here?

This is not just a case of one bad decision. This is a very familiar case of attitudes, which insist that Black folk are mere criminals who rightfully belong in prisons. Paramount to the judges and their bogus convictions is my point of taking our communities, our youth and our families to a whole 'nother level. We must maintain a level of conviction in that we refuse to allow such to happen to us. What is it that we will stand on and fight for? The wrongful and imbalanced convictions in the courtroom will cease to exist when we foster an unwavering belief to fight against malicious mindsets. Most significant is not just the belief in so doing, but an action agenda of how we shall go about saving the lives others aim to destroy.

For the brothers and sisters already incarcerated and serving unjust sentences, please continue to trust your personal conviction that is far greater than your imprisoned conviction. Continue to fight for your freedoms firmly with devout dedication to your innocence. For those of us outside the jail walls, we must stop living behind the psychological bars of fear. Have you ever stopped to realize that we are the true and honest answer to our very own prayers? Here's the legitimate verdict, the verdict of truth; our rightful convictions couched in courage will defeat these wrongful convictions of cowardice any day. I am convinced and convicted! I know that the freedom for our brothers and sisters wrongfully convicted is connected to our strength to stand with genuine conviction. We need not wait on freedom any longer; our convictions shall lead us to freedom that awaits us. This level of thinking really isn't about thinking at all; it is a convicted faith on "a whole 'nother level."

-NINE-
◇X◇

[Black Leadership]

Photo courtesy of Jamel Shabazz

FROM 2PAC TO BARACK:
A LETTER TO
THE HIP-HOP GENERATION

This is a story of what moved the Civil Rights Movement and why the movement is still necessary; yet this is no story. This letter addresses the lived experiences of a people constantly hung from trees of injustice. While it is often most convenient to tell these as stories to the tune of fiction, it is critical to address the realities of Black folk in a place such as America. Here we focus on this wealthy country that audaciously smothered and suffocated Black folks in its halls of poverty, discrimination, and inferiority, while demanding that we must be patriotic. It is here we call to question a post-racial conversation that ignores the need for post-racial character. It is my generation that has to critically think about and challenge the myth of racism being a thing of the past when we are still racially defined in jail cells and racially denied in classrooms.

From the shores in chains to segregated lunch counters, Black folk relentlessly fought for their freedoms. Many of us died unnecessary deaths with modest desires to simply live with dignity. Admittedly, the battles fought over the years rendered substantial gains in once segregated and unequal arenas such as public facilities and universities. Still today, despite such advancement, we find ourselves lagging educationally and losing spiritually. Far too many within inner cities are socially oppressed, thus emotionally depressed. The thinking on the horizon that insists, "all things are equal" is shameful. I contend the only "equal" thing to date is the very thinking that demanded a movement in the first place. Like that of the past century, there exists a thinking equal to that of White superiority and Black inferiority.

Rev. Dr. Martin Luther King, Jr. suggested that we can legislate policy but we cannot legislate attitudes. The challenge on this side of the Civil Rights Movement is thus our attitude, our way of thinking. In all of its success, the Civil Rights Movement could not shift the thinking of many American citizens. It is this unresolved and seldom addressed issue that today promotes imbalanced laws that substantially incarcerate the very youth we pay little to educate. How can a child dream of success when living nightmares of failure?

Today's inner-city communities demand a different type of movement. Too often we ask what happened to a people that once built pyramids? What happened to our people that marched and protested for justice and equality? What happened? Well, no other ethnic group contends with a history such as ours in America. No other group has been denied the right to read or write while they were establishing and maintaining a trillion-dollar economy, free of charge. No other ethnic group in America wrestles to find its face in history books. Our children today suffer from loss of identity. No other generation within our culture has had to contend with crack-cocaine, jails for profit, HIV/AIDS, abandoned buildings, abandoned children, vacant lots and vacant thinking.

Today's movement demands a new way of thinking about what it is we are trying to move. I contend that it starts with a discussion greater than a civil right. Our movement must deal with that of the spirit and the mind. What we are dealing with in many of our communities comes down to the heart of a people that is bruised and broken. What we are faced with as a people is the fact that we are not monolithic. We obviously do not think the same nor do we act the same; yet there are some things we desire which are the same. It is here where I park the point of Tupac and Barack. It is these two individuals as Black men who will drive home my point.

President Obama, referenced here as "Barack," debatably represents the success of the movement. Tupac, on the other hand, represents and lays to lyrics the failures of the movement. Barack's accomplished run for presidency calls for "change." Tupac depicts how things are yet the same. It is Barack that fights for peace in the world while Tupac insist he is "against the world." Tupac and Barack together represent a great divide within Blacks America to date; yet both are leaders for many of America's citizens. Ultimately, it is their thinking adjoined to their lived experiences in America that separates them.

Blackademically Speaking, I believe that there are those who think America can change and those who question such change. It is from this space we analyze the new movement. It is this nucleus that positions Barack as president to fight and end the Afghanistan war on behalf of America, as Tupac fights an Afghanistan-like war within himself because of America. Realistically, we must now contend with the many who suffer and benefit because of Whiteness in America. This is the disease. This is not a new   argument; it is simply unpopular to many. It is this point that demands fresh eyeglasses on how we see the ideologies of both Tupac and Barack. As Tupac says in his song, "Me Against the World," "the power is in the people and politics we address."

THE LIFE AND DEATH
OF RACISM

It is simply irresponsible, shameful and unacceptable to ignore racism as if it is a thing of the past. The Civil Rights Movement did not eliminate racism. In fact, many could argue that the attitudes remained the same, as laws and policies precariously shifted. Further, there has to be acknowledgment of the fact that racist behavior is simply not limited to United States citizens sporting white robes. Truth is, it was no more about the white robe than it was about the attitude of the human being clothed in the white robe. The Ku Klux Klan symbolically and with uniformity dressed in those robes, but it was their attitude that proved to be most destructive.

In that, it is very important for Black leadership to examine their attitudes as many gangbang for a false sense of power. Likewise, too many Black folk in leadership positions speak callously against others who recognize 21st century racism and racist behavior. For today, racism is not just individualized behavior or meager comments aimed at other groups outside the dominant culture of the U.S. It has often been defined in more complex ways. Author and activist Stokely Carmichael (*Black Power,* 1967), had this to say on the matter over 40 years ago:

> Racism is both overt and covert. It takes two, closely related forms: individual whites acting against individual Blacks, and acts by the total white community against the Black community. We call these individual racism and institutional racism...

{Institutional racism} is less overt, far more subtle, less identifiable in terms of specific individuals committing the acts. But it is no less destructive of human life... (it) originates in the operation of established and respected forces in the society, and thus receives far less public condemnation than the first type. When white terrorists bomb a Black church and kill five black children, that is an act of individual racism, widely deplored by most segments of the society. But when in that same city-Birmingham, Alabama-five hundred black babies die each year because of the lack of proper food, shelter and medical facilities, and thousands more are destroyed and maimed physically, emotionally and intellectually because of conditions of poverty and discrimination in the black community, that is a function of institutional racism. When a black family moves into a home in a white neighborhood and is stoned, burned or routed out, they are victims of an overt act of individual racism which many people will condemn-at least in words. But it is institutional racism that keeps black people locked in dilapidated slum tenements, subject to the daily prey of exploitative slumlords, merchants, loan sharks and discriminatory real estate agents. The society either pretends it does not know of this latter situation, or is in fact incapable of doing something meaningful about it.

Overwhelmingly, racism is conveniently ignored and largely misunderstood in mainstream America. A lack of education on the issue aids in many misunderstanding their own racist behavior and attitudes. It is quite comfortable to avoid critical and historical teaching on the subject. This is admittedly futile philosophy for a country deeply troubled by this issue. Ignoring something so gravely important means inviting our own demise. All the more devastating is the language of Blacks who themselves dismiss racism as old news despite what is happening in many communities of color. This is not to say that an individual cannot consider racism less important or, for that matter, unimportant. It is to say, however, that those Black folk, particularly in leadership, who adamantly speak in favor of racist policies, actions and attitudes, need to be ashamed of themselves. Clearly, they missed the memo on the heritage that helped materialize their very success. Without the plight of those before us, fighting racism none of us would be what we are or where we are today. Now, when others maintain that there is no need to discuss this topic as if it is absent in America's culture, I ask how absent is this evil considering the many individuals still subjected to it?

Oxygen is an unseen yet beneficial element that we need to survive. Gravity, although invisible to the eye as well, has a remarkable ability to keep many of us grounded. When is the last time you physically witnessed with your eyes the nitrogen largely composing the air we so desperately need for survival? Things that are invisible are not necessarily irrelevant nor are they ineffective. In fact, the opposite is largely possible and often true. Racism even as an "unseen" reality does not cancel out its effectiveness. Consider this:

Have you ever forgotten something and you knew in your mind what you were trying to say? It is a most disturbing reality to have your brain sort of lock down on you. You know what you are trying to say; you just at that moment cannot recall it. You then ask another for their assistance in shaping your point, and the best you can do is come close to what you initially wanted to say, though that is still not really the exact point you intended to make. Institutionalized racism helps us to identify what we want to say. Many are unable to call it because it is not in their vocabulary and ideological understanding. It is, nonetheless, largely responsible for the social impediments and injustices in America today. Judges that sit on corrupt benches, landlords that refuse parity to all of their tenants and police officers that mishandle their posts all represent racist behavior and thus perpetuate institutionalized racism.

Much of America's leadership has buried the term itself as they precariously resurrect new racist thoughts and ways of being. Various forms of racism are conveniently ignored in today's society because so many would rather attend its funeral. Burying racism is much easier than dealing with its rather healthy lifestyle accounting for its long life. What keeps racism alive are its healthy parents of White supremacy and Black inferiority. These great parents come from an ancestry of accomplished entities promoting values and morals with long-term intergenerational effects. Their marriage is a rather important union as neither could dare to live without the other. From my vantage point, in fact, they embody what true love really is.

Black inferiority in giving birth to Racism and Consciousness experienced some complications in her birth but these twins, looking nothing alike were both healthy. Oddly, despite the healthy household this loving couple provided, Consciousness ran away hating the comfort they provided for Racism. Treated as a stepchild, she vowed to never return and refused to be like her brother or her parents. After later meeting and marrying Spirit, they had many children. Consciousness named her triplets Knowledge, Wisdom and Understanding as they were the oldest of the bunch. Later came Intelligence, Love, Faith, Hope, Mercy, Longsuffering, Peace, Ambition and the baby Grace. Depending on where I find myself, I hear little of Consciousness and Spirit's lifestyle. Yet, whenever I do, they are always doing great.

As for Racism, well, I hear he married Prejudice and they too had many, many children. Perhaps their loving parents, in their love for god, were blessed with strong fertility genes. I am unable to call out all of their children names as I try to block them out considering the evil that they do to the many they encounter. However, I do know the oldest children. Racism insists on carrying on his name, giving birth to Racism II. He was given two sets of twins whom he named after his parents Black Inferiority and White Supremacy. Born in the middle of the sets of twins was Institutionalized Racism. The other set of twins, whom he mysteriously named Ni**a and Ni**er, seem out of place in their naming. I cannot imagine these two would ever like their names since they sound rather bizarre. I laugh because Racism, affectionately known as "Racist" as I make the distinction between he and his son, claims the names come from the Spanish language. He believes that they would be strongest in carrying out the power of their grandparents White Superiority and Black Inferiority. Only time will tell, I guess.

One thing is certain; Consciousness has nothing to do with any of them. Unable to choose her family members, she chose those who knew that Racism was nowhere close to breathing its last breath; it was the life that Racism has lived through its family members which forever chokes its chances of death.

SCHOLARVISM:
THE GATES OF OPPORTUNITY

One of the most intriguing scholarship programs sweeping the nation is that of Gates Millennium Scholars. As part of the inaugural class ten years ago, I have witnessed firsthand the existent talent pool of "minority" students in this nation. Each year, the program proudly selects 1000 qualified high school seniors and boldly provides full scholarships toward their college careers.

I often mention that God's grace and opportunity were intricately connected to my scholastic and academic success. As major threats confront affirmative action-based programs, Gates Scholars further validate what is attainable with just an opportunity. With the generous gift of Bill Gates to the United Negro College Fund, the program has helped thousands graduate, some achieving multiple degrees. Worthy of major analysis, however, is the act of service behind Bill Gates and his contribution to America's future. Considering the communities many of us represent, it is substantially crucial that there is a level of activism with our work as scholars — this I label scholarvism.

For decades, Black folk were denied opportunities to attain academic diplomas and degrees in America's schools. Their fight against such injustice often led to their own demise. In the courtrooms of America, various battles were fought for a right to the classrooms in America. As battles were lost and won, the war against Black folk heightened. Through it all, irrespective of where one stood ideologically, politically and personally, the resilience of underrepresented ethnic groups in America took form.

The challenge for many young scholars today is as great as yesterday's challenges albeit a different face. Many scholars of color opting for research relevant to their lives and communities are forced to rethink their research agendas in the name of rigor. For many, this challenge is fundamentally insulting as those who oppose such research, are often the very folk responsible for the oppression the scholars seeks to analyze. It is this attitude amongst dominant groups that demand a new type or scholar.

It is oddly more and more "unnecessary" to speak out against injustices. The smokescreen is centered on the accomplishments made over the years. This, at best, masks the current issues that are still very prevalent. It is unacceptable to consent to a changed conversation when so many of the issues are unchanged in their effect. Scholarvism demands relevant research adjoined to astute activism. This is not just the case for young, talented academicians seeking to someday influence policy, do research or stand as a professor or teacher in classrooms. This is an alert for all scholars afforded opportunities to enter colleges in this nation. The work is real and we must get real about this work. College degrees mean little if they are not utilized to change the fabric of foolishness used to comfort age-old ideologies. America lags the world educationally because too many have become stakeholders in wealth with little desire to serve those who lack such wealth. It is as though they skipped kindergarten, never learning the value of sharing.

After years of fighting and clawing, our ancestors battled for us to get to a place of decency as human beings. This fight was hardly about obtaining a degree alone. Just as this fight today is not solely about such, we must work hard to produce in classrooms and simultaneously work to obtain positive results in our communities. I personally challenge those scholars of color to a hand of scholarvism. As these cards are dealt throughout America to potentially bluff those of us with the winning hand, it is imperative that we hold our ground. We must demand to see just what the spread really is as we up the ante, royally flushing toxic social injustices, inequities and disparities. Scholarvism courageously calls out politicians, professors and policymakers that hide behind poker faces of multiculturalism and diversity. Scholarvism is essential for today's college graduate and young professional seeking to change the game as we know it. Our communities need more than scholarship; we need activism in favor of love, peace and justice — In the name of Scholarvism I am all in, are you?

-TEN-

<>X<>

Entertainers & Athletes

[Black Superstars]

Photo courtesy of Jamel Shabazz

T.I.P. Don't Let It Go to Your Head

"Daddy, if any man is to teach me how to play chess, it's gonna be you!" Laughing, he said in response, "Oh, now you want to learn how to play chess?" Throughout my childhood years, I watched my daddy literally destroy folk in the game of chess. He would study the board in the same way he demanded my brother and I study our books. As he contemplated moves, he would move his fingers over the pieces as some magician. It was not surprising all these years later to witness these same mannerisms. As he sat here at my place for the first lesson, he explained each piece and their viable moves on the board. The more he spoke, the more I questioned my Ph.D. As I laughed at him I blurted, "Daddy, you wanna slow down? I'm a beginner." His response was indicative of the woman I was proud to be as a result of he and my mom, "Just listen, you'll catch on." The more he spoke, the more I shook my head and borderline demanded that he slow down.

As I sat there honing in on his instructions, I figured it was my listening skills that were the problem. I intently listened all the more and came to the conclusion as to why I was hardly attracted to this board of small squares and funny looking pieces; it was complicated! It was just too much for me to take in and remember. As I felt discouragement come over me I recall saying, "Daddy, this is going to take some time." He agreed and we confirmed our weekly lessons for each Tuesday.

After going through a book I owned which taught the fundamentals of the game, coupled with the computerized version on my system, he gave me the homework for how to revisit his lessons in his absence. Little did I know that this absence would be long term, as that was my first and last full lesson with Daddy. He made his transition on a Tuesday afternoon, June 22, 2010.

> No coincidences — checkmate!
> GOD is real — checkmate!
> Grieve but Believe — checkmate!

After conflicting schedules and many missed Tuesday lessons, my dad and I agreed to start the summer off right. Tuesday, June 1, 2010, we arranged to meet. Oddly, in honor of my request, my daddy cleaned my carpet that day in lieu of our lessons. We talked and laughed, reminiscing on many things as he worked. After well over three hours, he left and we vowed to convene the following Tuesday. After returning to my place, in walking him to his car, I noticed he left his hat. I sent a text notifying him of such and said I would get it to him. Three weeks to the day later, my father made his transition — checkmate!

Within days of this heart-wrenching reality and en route to the funeral home to view the body, I drove as I often do without music playing. Strangely, this time I continued to blurt out, "Don't let it go to your head, no, don't let it go to your head, no, no, no, no." After about three to four times of so doing, I asked my cousin, "Why is that song in my head like that?" At which she replied, "I don't know." That moment was so strange as I had not heard the song in some time nor was it in my playlist of songs. "Was it one of your daddy's favorite songs?" asked my cousin. "What song wasn't," I replied in heavy laughter.

That night at my aunt's house, after several long hours and various conversations amongst family and friends, I was ready to depart. My cousin suggested otherwise and insisted that I stay longer. While in conversation with her, I mentioned that God had been strengthening me throughout this grieving process. I said to her that I felt a level of intimacy with God unlike before. God made me clear that I could grieve only as I believed. It was a strong point in that God's presence was very clear to me and the mandate of grieving, as I believed became my mantra. So if I believed that God was real, I must grieve as such. Oddly, the more I grieved, the more I reminded myself of what I truly believed and knew.

In talking to her, I told her of my daddy's last visit to my place and the sadness that was before me minus his presence now, in teaching me to play chess. I then told her how he had left his hat at my place.

As I shared my sentiments with her, I felt the Spirit all the more. It was beginning to make sense. To her I then said, "Wow, don't let it go to your head." As she listened, I knew she too made the connection, as this was the very woman, my cousin, in the car with me earlier. Now the question was being answered as to why this song was playing in my head.

Five years ago, my granddaddy Maurice Gill, Sr. made his transition. He was a Los Angeles Dodgers fanatic, which I did not completely understand until recently when I concluded it was possibly due to Jackie Robinson, a Dodger, being the first African-American to disrupt the racial barrier in the Major Leagues of Baseball. Nonetheless, when he passed on I expressed to my aunt that I simply desired his LA Dodgers cap.

When connecting these truths for my cousin's listening ear, the Spirit felt all the more powerful. I was witnessing the power of my biological daddy from another dimension. I was growing in hearing my Royal daddy spiritually too. I later insisted that my daddy would not rest in peace, as this was automatic in that he knew God and, surely, in being with God, he would rest. No, my daddy was now to Teach In Peace (T.I.P.). In peace he rested and now in peace he would teach his firstborn to teach others — checkmate!

My daddy's hat was left for me consistent with the hat I desired of his father and namesake. So there I stood speaking as the Spirit led, explaining to my cousin the clarity I was getting, "Don't let it go to your head, no, don't let it go to your head, no, no, no, no." See, my pastor from my college days said to me that he had learned from an elder, "To always wear the same-sized hat." In other words, no matter how high you go, never get the big head. This wisdom poured itself into this conversation as the connecting point — checkmate!

Two of the most important men in my life and their hats now reminded me, "to always wear the same-sized hat." It was no accident that my daddy, in his last visit to my home, physically left his hat. It was my reminder of his last visit of laughter, reminiscing and life-centered conversation that, through it all, I should never get a big head. One sure way to wear the same-sized hat is to be King-dom centered. In keeping the King on your dome, in your head (and heart), you remain grounded in what you are only as a result of God, our King.

To all the superstars, know this: what the world offers is nothing like honoring what God provides. It is, in fact, this world that affirms the lie of you being you because of you. The truth is that all you have and all that you are is because of God and His love for us, His children. It is thus all for His glory. Our communities suffer all the more in that we fail to acknowledge the very God who has brought us this far. This gross generalization does not encompass our entire race, as there are many who "wear the same-sized hat." Yet, this is a word for those who have not fully accepted, "To whom much is given, much is required." Perhaps we have not best understood that we are all only as strong as our weakest link. That which we have and own should be best utilized for those in need. There is no separating your skills and the reward of such athletically, from the many struggling individuals needing your assistance personally. There is no disconnecting your gift musically, from the mandate to rap, sing and dance positively, beyond some form of entertainment socially.

The Hip-Hop group Brand Nubian and their remake of Jean Carne's song, "Don't Let it Go to Your Head," says:

> "Lot of people often ask, 'Puba, how you givin' back?'
> The way I give back is through the knowledge of my raps."

Our world is in turmoil. If our world is in turmoil and we are lagging the world academically, for instance, then truly our communities are in greater turmoil. I often say that we are behind the behind. Our superstars must know that nothing about solely entertaining the world is super, particularly if we degrade our culture on the world stage.

The wealthy moguls of our time, the athletes, the college-educated graduates, the actors, actresses, attorneys and other professionals must not let it go to their heads. Acknowledging the Super God that we serve, best prevents us from running the risk of getting the big head. Our communities would be a much greater place if the common folk knew just how super they really were and if the superstars knew they were just common.

One of Hip-Hop's pioneering female artists, MC Lyte, says:

"In between lives I'm so confused,
What do I do, oh, what do I do?"

In this, her song released decades ago, "Cappuccino," MC Lyte tells the story of her experience with this drink. This "dream" stems from the power of Cappuccino in which she is left feeling "confused." Today, one of the most popular places to meet and drink Cappuccino is in Starbucks. This international coffeehouse sells in high volume what MC Lyte helped introduce our younger communities to, and so I argue and insist that, as the star, she made the bucks. Her popularity extended well beyond this song as a lyricist. Arguably one of the greatest female artists, her talent was evident and her lyrical question here is profoundly prophetic. MC Lyte's question of what to do is for the current-day superstar and the answer is:

As Jean Carne said, "Don't let it go to your head." As my
pastor said, "Wear the same-sized hat. As I can now say,
"We don't need stars who just make the bucks."

That last conversation with my daddy on June 1, 2010 ended in my place with me saying to him that I just wanted to serve God and do His will. To that my daddy smiled. Perhaps his purpose was fulfilled. Maybe he felt in his inner soul, he had done God's will and his joy was in hearing me say the same. Truly, I feel God all the more and His Spirit clarified my daddy's hat left behind. As I complete this essay with his hat on my head, I say, "Daddy, continue to T.I.P. Checkmate, you are now with the real King!"

I BEAR WITNESS TO WHITENESS: THE KING JAMES EFFECT

Like many school graduating classes, the year 2003 for the NBA was pivotal and memorable to say the least. Emerging as arguably one of the greatest draft classes in NBA history, this class of athletes would indirectly and finally swing the pendulum from what many in my generation deemed the league of Michael Jordan. This new class of talent emerged as the best in the league with today's stars in the likes of Carmelo Anthony, Chris Bosh, Dwyane Wade and, of course, LeBron James. For the many individuals who could care less about sports, the truth is few could successfully escape the infamous and public impact of LeBron James.

Despite Kobe Bryant's major success in the league as an NBA champion and an overall dominant player, many argued that the league's prominence had waned. As many battled what was contentiously a major loss in the giant of Michael Jordan as superstar and phenom to the league, few I believe saw the class of talent on the horizon that would not only shift the league's level of stardom and talent, but too would ultimately challenge and change the business savvy of its athletes.

LeBron James as the #1 pick in 2003's draft class has since emerged as one of the most powerful and prominent athletes in sports. In so doing, his recent decision to leave his own hometown of Akron, Ohio created not only a buzz, but also led many to question his loyalty to the sport and ultimately the very city he was raised in. Having entered the league as a high school graduate, he immediately created wealth for himself. Emerging into stardom as a young teenager, his nearly $100 million deal from Nike alone was substantially voluminous and this was just the beginning.

What happens to a game or sport when the players begin to recognize their monetary value to the very sport itself? When is it too much? Why is there so much contention over the decision of LeBron James? Is this a case in which Blacks, as players, are to stay in their place for their White owners?

Currently, there is only one African-American held team, owned by none other than Michael Jordan. While ownership amongst Blacks in all major sports in America is a real issue, the majority of the NBA's players are Black. The ownership reality in the NBA is, at best, insulting. As we continue to learn here, for too long, Blacks have had to play catch-up in a country that has long denied us the very access to power and wealth. The inherent issue here is Whiteness.

Whiteness in America is seldom referenced, especially in this context. Like that of racism, these terms are often swept under the rug and conveniently ignored. Whiteness privileges White people in not having to think about race and its effects. It is Whiteness that has long been the standard in America. Many individuals have fallen prey to Whiteness not even knowing what to name it. For instance, Black students are often compared to White students and criticized for not being as intelligent or smart. People in America are often relegated to blonde (long) hair and blue eyes as beautiful. White is pure and Black is filthy. Part of what is associated with Whiteness is a spirit of arrogance when one is White. This leads to other races struggling to be White or, if nothing else, marrying and befriending Whites for an underlying and sole purpose of connecting to what has been presented as great. For Whites, there is a comfortable connection in being a part of the very group that is dominant, powerful and even beautiful. On many accounts, Whiteness in America is a not-so-silent killer.

Specific to the NBA, Whiteness has taken its dominant seat of power in the stands of arrogance. Consider the arrogance of our sports establishment when it happily credits its champions as World Champions although having played against and defeating only our own. Clearly, the NBA is best known around the world as the greatest and most prestigious professional league of basketball. Yet, from a global standpoint, the U.S. has lost its savvy in a more competitive basketball world during the past decade.

In facing this increased competition, the U.S. finished sixth in 2002 and in 2004 as the Summer Olympic team lost three games on its way only to a bronze medal. They would only win bronze in 2006 as well. Although they redeemed the gold in 2008 and 2010, the obvious reality is that the NBA players often comprising the Olympic basketball teams lost their global dominance. With this in mind, it is imperative that we analyze how the NBA generates a "World" champion despite America's actual losses against other teams in the world.

In understanding these things, we find that Whiteness in America has shaped much of America's cases made against the newer talent, like that of LeBron. I find it nothing short of ironic how Black players are asked to be loyal to a sport or, in this case, a city which, in turn, is not obligated to do the same. The game of basketball is not just a sport when it comes to the NBA, quite the contrary. It is a game played at an optimum level in an industry that generates billions of dollars globally. Simply put, it is a business.

Choose to understand how it must feel to have an entire nation on your team, rooting for you, supporting you and protecting you till the end whether you win or lose-this is Whiteness. Said plainly, it is like those growing up in the 'hood having none to bully you because of your connection to a large family in that very neighborhood. To mess with you is to ask for problems from the many in your family. You walk through your neighborhood with arrogance realizing that, despite the woes of your community at large, you will never or hardly experience such because of who had your back. Well, with Whiteness, White people have been privileged in America having their back.

The effect that LeBron has on the game athletically should be matched with respect for him socially and even how he handles his business professionally. Those in critique of his decisions as a business man, should question whether Black or White, if they are a fan of Whiteness or a supporting "witness" to LeBron's emerging style. And this is not about the race card, Whiteness in America is about who always holds the cards, oftentimes stacks the cards and yet on the horizon are those like LeBron who seek to unstack the cards against them; thus, we bear "witness" to the diminishing Whiteness of it all — Go 'Bron!

THE HAVES AND HAVE-NOTS

As poverty hits an unprecedented high in America, the recession continues to prove its massive effects. Long before the financial disturbance, however, there existed a spiritual debt in this country. The bail-out for the few with large bank ($$$) contributed to the foreclosed faith of so many left with little to bank on. As Americans continue to wait on the effects of the government approved stimulus package, their hope is left bankrupt and their invested stock of belief in America constantly diminishes.

As teachers fight for respectable wages here in America, multi-million dollar contracts are signed daily for athletes, entertainers, actors, actresses, etc. While there is no crime in rewarding young men and women for their talents on courts, fields and the big screen, there is room for critical conversation and discussion on our value of educators and education as significant and important.

Mayor Han Zheng of Shanghai, China considers teaching a prestigious position; perhaps this is why teachers in Shanghai, earns just as much money as medical doctors.

Just as impressive, their teachers heavily populate math and science fields. Despite a population of over 20 million people, Shanghai maintains an awesome ability to produce sound educational results.

According to PISA (Program for International Student Assessment), America significantly lags Shanghai, which recently received the top international test scores in math, science and reading. In fact, America is almost the farthest behind Shanghai. Of the 34 countries belonging to the OECD (Organization for Economic Cooperation and Development), America ranked 25th in math, 17th in science, and 14th in reading. Despite more than doubling what we spend per pupil, in recent decades our test scores remain flat. Further, our best and brightest students are unable to compete with students in Singapore, Hong Kong, South Korea, Taiwan, and Japan. So what do we make of this specific to who gets what in America and what all of this means globally?

Make no mistake about it; all of our youth are not caught in this web of choosing rap songs and playing ball over professions like that of teaching. Nor is it wrong for those interested in sports or music to choose careers, pursuing such dreams. The emphasis here is on the responsibility we have as a country on what we put the emphasis of prestige on. This is about those that have and those that have not. What will we make of this and all of its domestic and global implications? What message does this send to Black America, specifically?

Throughout history, African-American communities have valued the success of those within their reach. Black folk heavily applaud those that "make it." In contrast, those reaching levels of success, feel the pressure of not only trying to help so many, but also they find themselves filling voids of poverty they experienced their entire lives. Entertainers in videos are notorious for showing the world their possessions while seeming to pay little attention to their growing obsession for even more of those things. Sadly, this attitude trickles down to their fans that often look like them and soon aspire to be just like them.

The sparked controversy behind Charles Barkley saying, "I am not a role model" generated much conversation in the 90's. Here you have a world-famous basketball star telling parents everywhere that he was not looking to "raise your kids." For many, this was seen as rude or disrespectful. How could he say such a thing? Why would he send this message? What the media did not highlight were his additional words centered on just how few could actually become basketball players. This point was extremely significant. As many young people aspire to play basketball, how many are truly prepared for a college environment and playing on a collegiate level? Further, how many will qualify for the extremely selective drafts of these world-class leagues?

As Blacks in America continue to make gains in respective fields, off the field throughout America there must be an answer to the call of being a role model. While Black folk are not a monolithic people, meaning that we do not all think the same, feel the same or act the same, there are issues that impact us just the same. As we push for more ownership with hopes of building equity for our next generation's future, we must willingly take the baton. In running the race, we must humbly acknowledge how we got here in the first place. Our sole motto must be a tribute to the role models before us: All that we have today is in sharp contrast to what so many had not yesterday.

Few could argue the courage of Bill Russell, Jim Brown or even Althea Gibson, the first Black in professional tennis. It was Althea Gibson that paved the way for Arthur Ashe and the Williams sisters of the day. It was Althea Gibson, who said:

> "In the field of sports you are more or less accepted for what you do, rather than what you are," and "No matter what accomplishments you make, somebody helped you."

Today's superstars are not just on the basketball court, but they are also lawyers and judges representing justice in legal courts. Today's role models are willing men and women that play on tennis and football fields and those with multiple degrees in various fields of study. Today's superstars are the youth that discipline themselves as they sharpen their talent to sing, dance or play sports as well as the youth seeking Ph.D.'s in disciplines such as social science or natural science.

For those that have not, I say this, stop focusing on what you do not have and work with what you do have; in working with what you already have you will soon obtain what you have not now. This is not just about what you desire to be when you "grow up." This is about having ambition. Ambition is a strong desire to possess, own and achieve. Who has the ambition of being that role model? Who will take on the role of mentoring our youth in our communities? Know this, our work is not charity. It is our obligation to do these things because those who came before us successfully accomplished the same while having much less than what we have.

We cannot donate our way out of our troubled situations. Writing a check each month is okay, but it is the works alongside the check that will help empty the jail cells and street corners while filling classrooms. In order to have what matters spiritually, we must first bankrupt ourselves of selfishness, greed, ignorance and arrogance. Our line of credit as a community will increase substantially if we are willing to pay the interest of being courageous, sacrificial and faithful. God's return on such investment has nothing to do with Wall Street; our investments as superstar role models will result in enhancing the value of our own streets.

This is the memo to Black America, as said earlier; if the best of America is behind the brightest in the world and we are behind in America, what are we to say of our fight educationally? Thirty years ago, Shanghai was not the powerhouse it is today. In thirty years it reformed its educational system. In fact, thirty years ago, Shanghai had exactly one skyscraper. It now has close to 800. What's the memo to Black America? The same memo I provide to America: properly educating all students, even the have-nots, is vital to our future as a country and what we will have!

-ELEVEN-

◇×◇

Photo courtesy of Jamel Shabazz

THE $1,000,000,000,000 BLUNT

Some have reported that by 2012, African-American spending in America will peak at an astounding $1,000,000,000,000.00. Seems like a whole lot of zeroes from my end. Where is all this money coming from? Or better, where is it going? Why is it that our communities look as they do in so many parts of the country considering such an amount of money? Perhaps there are still some unidentified principles needed in our lives. One thing is certain; we must note that where we buy potato chips and a gallon of milk is a cultural statement. It is a statement centered on how we see or even value our future and ourselves. Think about the last transaction you made. Who did you give your money to? Who owns the grocery store you shop in? What about the gas stations you frequent? Your utility bills? When is the last time you had a conversation with an owner of one of these places about just where your money was going?

For many years there has been an outcry in Black communities about the importance of "buying Black." This has been spoken of in the hope that Blacks will experience economic empowerment. I have concluded that the idea is a grand one. Yet the problem for many of us is that we fail to see our empowerment being connected to our very own spending. Further, we have failed to learn the true art of investing. This art is centered on spending not only your money but also your time and energy with things that will provide a significant return for your future.

In my travels and in speaking to youth throughout the country, I have been overwhelmingly plagued by what is no longer a silent epidemic.

Marijuana is, of course, no new drug to any community, let alone the African-American community. Many have insisted in the usage of this social drug void of an examination of its effects. Further, as I have learned from far too many high school students and now elementary age students who engage, "it is something to keep your mind off of problems." Intrigued by the responses from 13- to 14-year-old boys, I have concluded that the silence and acceptance within our communities largely explains the ruin of our communities.

Black Wall Street in Tulsa, Oklahoma was as one of the greatest investments by Blacks for Blacks. This small community flourished as Oklahoma, a new state on the scene, began to establish itself in 1907. Known for having several Black millionaires and dozens of professionals, this community was armed with Black businessmen, doctors, lawyers, etc. Within this small community existed restaurants, grocery stores, schools, law offices, a bank, post office, libraries, etc., owned by Black people. This community boomed until the race riots of May 31 to June 1, 1921. Many stories have circulated about what really happened to erupt such violence in the Greenwood district of Tulsa. The Ku Klux Klan is on record as having a strong membership in the area. Pertinent here, however, are the 600 businesses lost in the area and the elimination of the Black community's infrastructure.

One hundred years later, here we stand unable to replicate the business model of Tulsa. Why? We have many more young professionals. We have greater access. We have much more money. So, what's the problem? Is it a problem? Economic empowerment is the best cultural statement we could ever make as a people. Choosing to invest in your future begins with an agenda centered on economics. I don't care how much you love your church and the pastor, if you cannot pay the bills of the church, you cannot worship in the church with your pastor. Quite frankly then, the very relationship we seek to establish among "Believers" on Sundays is oddly connected to economics.

Right now, communities in inner cities are being gentrified. Folks are being relocated. Ownership is central to the heart of this issue. We can no longer afford to solely rent and consume. We must own. I am disgusted at the long lines outside of local athletic shoe stores awaiting the arrival and sale of the newest gym shoes. We must demand more for ourselves beyond such superficial material. Liabilities are things that lose value and assets are things worth your investment. Clothes, shoes, cars, etc., are all liabilities. Assets are traditionally associated with land, for instance, which has greater potential of generating revenue. After you purchase a jogging suit, not only will it not render a return on your investment, it is something you will wear less and less over a longer period of time.

The truth is we must be individually responsible. The investment in things as assets is just as critical as the investment of your time in discovering your purpose. Invest your energy instead of smoking away your energy. As you smoke, we all pay. Your financial investment in a blunt is a cultural investment in nothingness. Each hour of the day is critical. Time is something you will never get back. Consider for a moment how often you smoke and think about this: I began taking Phenobarbital at the tender age of 13 years old. This medication was needed to treat my seizure activity as an epileptic. I had to take six pills each day, three in the morning and three in the evening. The milligrams (mg) ranged from 30-60mg per tablet. At best, over the years my doctor would allow a lower dosage.

I decided I wanted to review my options in ridding myself of this drug as I began to feel that the drug was doing more harm than good. After speaking with a few physicians, I learned that I could wean myself slowly. I thus searched for alternative methods to traditional Western medicine. I was determined to live beyond these doctors' orders. I changed my lifestyle again in deciding to eat even healthier and work out more. I dedicated myself to preserving myself. Almost two years ago, I took my last pill. The truth is, though, that twenty years of my life were spent consuming this drug. I recall my weaning myself from the drug and the feeling I would get. I later learned that it was not my body needing the drug per se, but my body's response in withdrawal from the drug. After twenty years I realize I have taken over 40,000 pills and nearly 2,000,000 *mg* of that very drug. Considering the fact that this drug was *necessary* in preventing my seizure activity, I, of course, would have had it no other way. Yet, for those smoking weed, green, etc., I challenge you in thinking about the cost.

Your consumption of this drug is greater than a moment with your street-corner "homies." In fact, your consumption is a liability to your family and your future. It is yet one more thing you consume at the mercy of productivity. Choose today to reevaluate your priorities. Let us invest in turning this thing around one blunt at a time. First, what we must do as a community of champions is admit we have problems. Our problem is an addiction to consumerism. We will consume any and everything as long as we look good and "high" doing it. The cultural pay off of such is ultimately a spiritual bankruptcy I do not believe any of us can afford.

Get your mind right! Step up your game. Rid yourself of this lousy addiction. The drug is the addiction and consumerism is yet another of our silent killers. In the end it is all the same because, when you're high, you can't even see the smoke screen. The reality is that you are paying for the very drug that keeps you as high as the price you are paying for very low results in your life. So, how much are you willing to pay for your liberation from this addiction?

PURCHASED POVERTY

"May I have a number 10 and can you please SUPER-size it"? There is nothing greater than placing an order for something you have longed for all day. Well, there is one thing greater and that is being able to super-size it. The fast food industry has over the years gained much notoriety for its swiftness in delivering your meal. Unlike fast food chains, more upscale restaurants have food in house and generally prepare food per your order. Either way, the consumer pays for services provided.

Coupled with our theme regarding consumerism and investments, is the needed discussion regarding costs. Let's examine this: there is a desired product on sale for $149.99, half the original price. While the cost is 50% cheaper, the reality is that it is relative. Let's say the item you purchased is a video game you have so desired for your children. Yes, the item's price is perfect for this one-day sale. Yes, it is cheap, especially considering the regular amount of the console. However, what makes this all very relative are the critical questions we fail to ask in general. Is this a needed item or a desired one? Is it necessary to purchase now irrespective of the sale. Lastly, is this an investment for your children and their future?

In many households today, video games are the parents raising children. Flat screens with graphic television shows and MP3 players banging explicit lyrics, are now teaching our children. That $149.99 without tax is arguably a horrible purchase for children, particularly if they are failing in school. Far too many parents waste their money on the latest shoes, for instance, with a desire to maintain name brand status.

Truth is, those same funds are best used for educational materials that will enhance the quality of life for any child. To further the problem, we use over-the-limit, high interest credit cards to purchase such items. It is quite remarkable noticing the level of poverty within our communities, while acknowledging the wealth of materialistic items in our households.

We have to analyze culturally why it is we do what we do. We have, in a sense, purchased our own poverty. This addiction of consuming and not owning is to our detriment. We have before us a cultural crisis. Schools are unequally funded and thus inequitable. Jails and prisons thrive in the face of injustice. Politicians play political games, in their support of lopsided policies. The cultural cost of our personal neglect and lack of responsibility is huge. Look at it this way: it is not a sale you just bumped into or long awaited. It really is a **sell.** This is a new way of thinking about selling out. That item you purchased for sale, was a parental sell-out to your children and their needed development. I know this sounds harsh and rough, yet it is timely. The cultural cost is paid financially, socially, spiritually, psychologically, etc., in what we do not have as a people.

Blackademically Speaking, there is a need for us to shift our priorities. We must evaluate how and where we spend our money. Currently, we are contributing to the institutional debacle by purchasing our impoverished state. It is similar to purchasing a dilapidated and abandoned building, with no money for necessary repairs. Where you currently live, you pay rent as a tenant. Would you buy the vacant building? To what end is it valuable? Is the purchase significant? Is it important to say you have property, or is it intelligent to continue renting.

The purchase, from an investment standpoint, only makes sense if the goal is an immediate profit. Where is no such plan, the purchase is ludicrous. We buy just to buy with no contextual reasoning. We then own these liabilities at high risk to our communities and our own future—our children's future. After a while, our misguided purchase becomes an eyesore and useless. The impoverished mind has to change its focus. Abolitionist, and former slave, Frederick Douglass states:

> "If there is no struggle, there is no progress. Those who profess to favor freedom, and deprecate agitation, are men who want crops without plowing up the ground, they want rain without thunder and lightning."

If we want financial freedom, we must do the work today. Stop your purchase of poverty. Rid yourself of the cultural cost we all pay, as a result of one's decisions. There is value in purchasing things to read, over rims for your car. There is value in choosing not to pay $5.00/gallon for gas, just to be seen in your local neighborhood rolling. There is a value associated with purchasing CD's over CD's. The CD that matters here are certificates of deposits. It is a low-risk investment with higher interest yields than a savings account and just lower than stock. Although they look the same, they are obviously quite different. One you purchase for listening pleasure, the other you purchase for long-term living pleasure.

> You: "Yes, I would like to order mis-education to go with a side order of purchased poverty. Oh, and can you please SUPER-size it?"

> Your Homie: "And for me, I will take a number of rims and dubs with just a large order of oppression; for dessert, I would like to have a small-sized book."

THEY THAT WEIGHT
ON THE LORD

What is it that you are waiting on God to do in your life? Did you make New Year's resolutions that are still unfulfilled? Do you find yourself making the same resolution again this year, because the past years have not been most productive in achieving that goal for you? Perhaps you should examine the process in how you are hoping to achieve that which you SAY is important to you. If you believe things will happen in your life for you, and thus without you, you are sadly mistaken.

One of the greatest challenges in life is centered on our inability to work hard for what we desire and even deserve. This is nothing new for mankind. For years many have actually preached the importance of waiting on God. I believe that waiting is essential as it is in spaces of waiting where God can best speak to us. When we settle in with the Lord and trust in His word, in this waiting period we can hear from Him in being led. Just as important is the fact of waiting with GOD and hearing from God as He carries the weight of your burden. In prayers with purpose, we come to God with the weight of our issues and we wait as God takes them from us.

Yet, what happens when you are waiting and without purpose? What happens when you wait with a purpose? If I say to you as my friend to "wait on me until I return," and I have a proven track record of not following through, would you wait? If I were that dependable friend asking you to wait five minutes as I run to get something, perhaps the wait isn't difficult. How many children are still waiting on their daddy to return after he promised he would "be right back"?

To wait is not the easiest of things to do. Yet, with reliable sources involved, it can be well worth it. God delivers on what He promises, particularly when divine purpose is involved. Unfortunately, from my assessment, this notion of waiting has become the very obstacle of our own development. Think about it. Here you sit wondering why you have not been able to lose the weight you said years ago you would lose. Why are you still overweight? Well, you are over**wait**, I surmise, because you are overly waiting on God to lose your wait for you; it is you that you need in getting it done! Frederick Douglass is our brother and a famous Black man who freed himself from slavery; he said the following:

> "I prayed for twenty years but received no answer until
> I prayed with my legs."

Frederick Douglass declared as an abolitionist that he was the answer the whole time; how about that? In his prayers he came to understand that his work, his movement and his activity were the answer to his own prayers. Can you imagine it, a slave on a plantation declaring this some 150 plus years ago? What he knew then, we should consider now. Sometimes the very thing we ask God to do, HE has already done. In fact, the irony is this: God is waiting on us! HE has already assigned us to do what He has called us to do. He's even strengthened us in the area of preparation and purpose. It is our fear that prevents us from fulfilling our destiny. I have come to believe this:

> We are overweight in our fears and anorexic in our faith.
> We are bloated in depression and bulimic in determination.

The bottom line is that we have been mis-educated on waiting, and as we wait there are so many others around us who work and take. Think about how much of our faith is centered on some traditional waiting game. We are taught to wait on our mates as God will send him/her to us. We are taught to wait on Him as we pray for that next job, the new career and our college acceptance. We have been trained to wait on the Lord for our deliverance and, thus, our own freedom. So, we wait on God to redeem us. We wait on Him to send an unexpected check in the mail for our long overdue bills. We even wait for that next year so we can file our income taxes again, only to receive them and wait all over again.

From my standpoint, waiting as we have come to know it has been most detrimental to our individual growth and development. At the nucleus of messages leaving the pulpit is the importance of "waiting on the Lord." In waiting on the Lord to return, "not knowing the day or the hour," many, many people have forsaken their own work. There they wait, "not knowing the day nor the hour," as opposed to working and preparing for that day and hour. The latter is critical because, in working to live as God says, we actually welcome His coming.

Associated with this thinking and lack of doing is a "faith" couched in urban communities that is affectionately deemed "chilling." No other ethnic group has been conditioned as Black folk in this area of waiting. Look around you. I dare you to visit other races and their cultural characteristics. Talk to Jews about their faith and how they do what they do. Seek their understanding of Jesus. I insist that no other race in America is left waiting on their empowerment and advancement. And I also insist that when we take on the attributes of working and not waiting, we become problematic. When Dr. King carried out his mission of non-violent protest, it was at its core a mission of working and not waiting. Despite popular thinking, his philosophy was not altogether weak. In fact, it was the opposite as it provoked White preachers, his own fellow clergymen of the cloth, who all insisted that he wait on his freedom. Dr. King responded this way, in his *Letter from Birmingham Jail, 1963*:

> We have waited for more than 340 years for our constitutional and GOD-given rights. The nations of Asia and Africa are moving with jet-like speed toward gaining political independence, but we still creep at horse-and-buggy pace toward gaining a cup of coffee at a lunch counter. Perhaps it is easy for those who have never felt the stinging darts of segregation to say, 'Wait.' But when you have seen vicious mobs lynch your mothers and fathers at will and drown your sisters and brothers at whim; when you have seen hate-filled policemen curse, kick, and even kill your black brothers and sisters; when you see the vast majority of your twenty million Negro brothers smothering in airtight cages of poverty in the midst of an affluent society; when you suddenly find your tongue twisted and your speech stammering as you seek to explain to your six-year-old daughter why she can't go to the public amusement park that has been advertised on television, and see tears welling up in her eyes when she is told that Funtown is closed to colored children, and see ominous clouds of inferiority beginning to form in her little mental sky, and see her beginning to distort her personality by developing an unconscious bitterness toward white people; when you have to concoct an answer for a five-

year-old son who is asking: 'Daddy, why do white people treat colored people so mean?'; when you take a cross country drive and find it necessary to sleep night after night in the uncomfortable corners of your automobile because no motel will accept you; when you are humiliated day in and day out by nagging signs reading 'white' and 'colored'; when your first name becomes 'nigger,' your middle names becomes 'boy' (however old you are) and your last name becomes 'John,' and your wife and mother are never given the respected title 'Mrs.' When you are harried by day and haunted by night by the fact that you are a Negro, living constantly at tiptoe stance, never quite knowing what to expect next, and are plagued with inner fears and outer resentments; when you are forever fighting a degenerating sense of 'nobodiness' — then you will understand why we find it difficult to wait. There comes a time when the cup of endurance runs over, and men are no longer willing to be plunged into the abyss of despair. I hope, sirs, you can understand our legitimate and unavoidable impatience.

Moreover, and most importantly, he declares:

For years now I have heard the word 'Wait!' It rings in the ear of every Negro with piercing familiarity. This 'Wait' has almost always meant 'Never.' We must come to see, with one of our distinguished jurists, that 'justice' too long delayed is justice denied.

So, what are you waiting on? The weight of our issues will not be resolved with us waiting. To lose this weight of problems in our inner-city communities, we have to take on the fear diet. We cannot wait another day. The champion in us must declare we will diet from fear and strengthen the muscles of faith.

-TWELVE-

◇X◇

Motivation Section

[Black People | Black Champions]

Photo courtesy of Dr. Chandra Gill

THERE MUST BE (AN) ALIGNMENT WITH MY ASSIGNMENT!

So many of us wander through life aimlessly and this is unnecessary. God has provided each of us the tools needed to fulfill the very calling He has on our lives. The challenge for us all is to connect with Him in such a way where we will know what that calling is. I refer to it as our assignment. What has God assigned you to do? What are you to accomplish while here on earth? When is the last time you spent time with God searching and trusting? What is your purpose?

Have you ever had a broken relationship? How did it make you feel? What came of it? A lack of productive communication is one of the largest reasons why many adults suffer in relationships. Be it we fail to communicate our infidelity, our mistrust or our pains, our hurts, our fears, it all amounts to the very point I am making here; relationships suffer most often because we fail to speak clearly about our attitudes and actions. We build walls keeping others out as opposed to building solid links in chains to bind others to us.

Such is the case for how we have treated God much of our lives. Despite His love for us, we have treated our relationship with Him with much negligence and lack. It is no wonder so many of us wander aimlessly through life, treating God's power like that of a crap game. God is no magician and He surely does not want you to crap out. Yes, He works miracles, yet that is different than rolling dice and pulling cats from hats. Here we are, approaching each day wondering and guessing and hoping as opposed to trusting and believing in what He has said. We have failed to see God as the powerful deity that He truly is. We trust little in what He can do because we have not the relationship needed to understand the essence of His greatness and supreme power.

Consider this: as a child, parents are to provide for your basic necessities, as it is improbable for you to have to do for yourself at such an age. As I have mentioned, my parents handled their responsibilities with respectable care. I do not recall a day where I would question if the lights would be on or if heat would warm our cold winter nights. In this I park my point. When I look back, I now know that it was never necessary for me to ask my parents before turning on lights whether they would come on. The heat was turned up without my wondering if the bill was paid. Even if my parents were to struggle in making ends meet, it was not my knowledge as it was customary for them to handle the business of the household as parents while my brother and I lived as their children.

I submit unto you that God is no different. As with our biological parents, He, as our Royal Father, provides for us. He never fails in showing us how much He loves us. He takes care of our needs and goes so far as to provide for us in spite of who we are and are not. We simply do not have to question a God that has a history of seeing to it that we are taken care of. He is not a negligent parent. If, in fact, we find ourselves at this moment questioning God, the problem is not with Him as provider; it is with us as His children.

Our relationship with God is essential to the fullness of our lives. The assignment for our lives is found in the communication with God who made our lives possible. It is ultimately found in and with our devotion to God. In His infinite wisdom, God has created each of us for a work He needs to be delicately done. Too much of our time is spent asking questions. Furthering this as a problem is the fact that we never get answers and we settle for this. This is unacceptable. There are answers and your life should not be lived as one big question mark. Instead of only asking questions, search for answers and choose to not give in until that answer is provided. This energy and shift in thinking will guide you to your ordained and divine destiny.

In my quiet time with God I have learned that we all have an assignment. Whereas one's calling and purpose are interconnected, they are uniquely different. To simplify, one's assignment in life involves an understanding of your calling specific to your purpose. How does one make sense of their life and what they are to do? My philosophy with respect to your assignment begets that childhood question, "What do you want to be when you grow up?" See, we hear early on remnants of the importance of our lives and our purpose. Yet, there is this apparent breakdown over time on how to live it out. This calling that I reference here is not solely your career as a doctor or teacher. The calling is connected to how God chooses to use you as a doctor or a teacher. Your assignment is in short, what you are to do and where you are to do it— notwithstanding doing it when it is supposed to be done.

Then there is this alignment. More times than none, there are those unable to speak to what their assignment is. Few know what they are truly called and purposed to do. The more simple aspect of this is your alignment. This is what I refer to as your gifts. What is it that God blessed you to do? What are you passionate about and great in seeing through? These gifts are not just talents. It is at the heart of what God connected to your purposeful calling. Your alignment is critical to your assignment. Your gifts are critical to your calling. They work hand in hand as your purpose in living and serving God. It is imperative that we see this for our lives.

Knowing your gifts void of understanding your purposeful calling is debatably detrimental. It is possible to know your gifts yet find yourself operating outside the way(s) they are to be used. Let's examine this as a closing point: Driving a vehicle in need of a wheel alignment is not impossible or completely hazardous. In fact, many have been known to drive despite such need. Clearly, over time this is problematic for the tires and other surrounding elements that take a beating because of the need to align the tires, yet the car is still drivable. The fullness of the vehicle's operation is satisfied with aligning the tires.

Like this vehicle, too many of us are riding through life in need of an alignment. We are coasting through life, settling for and accepting far less than what we deserve when there is far more to our existence. Many of us are out of alignment with God, thus, we are not clear on our gifts as they relate to our assignment. We must know both. It is a blessing to operate in your gift simultaneous to operating within your purposeful calling.

Nurture and properly use your gifts. Keep in mind that knowing your assignment is a privilege and necessary. For years I knew I had a gift of teaching. My "gift of gab" was the sure giveaway to this aspect of my calling. Yet in knowing this, I still found myself using my gift of gab in some of the wrong places. Sure, I can flow through life in such respects, yet the fullness of my life was not yet realized. Again, note that a car can still run with a need of a wheel alignment. The assignment requires the wheel alignment. It puts everything into proper place.

My purposeful calling is the assignment of where I am to be in using my gifts. I must seek to use them as ordered by God. I can, as I have, use my "gift of gab" in tearing people down as opposed to building people up. The alignment alone is simply not good enough. Our assignment best positions us. So then, we simply cannot afford to dismiss devotion with

God in search of our calling and our individual gifts. We must recognize the need for this alignment and assignment so that we can begin to change our lives, while we have these lives to live in the first place.

CHALLENGED AND CHANGED! SUCCESSFULLY

It is my position that we have yet to change because we refuse the challenge in so doing. We have heard over and over again that change is hard. We have, unfortunately, accepted this as truth. Sure, change is an adjustment, but what in life is not? Clearly, we had to adjust to new shoe sizes and clothing. There was a required adjustment to realizing that momma and daddy would no longer take care of us. Life is all about adjustments. Change is just that. We have viewed it as "hard" because of the effort we must put forth in making it a reality and, quite frankly, we just refuse to put in the work.

I learned long ago that, specific to urban communities, we refused to challenge ourselves regardless of our circumstances. Yes, as we have discussed throughout this book, life is no box of chocolates for many of us in how we have been forced to live in America. Yet, I submit here that the change we need is interwoven in the challenges we accept. It is altogether too common for people to suggest, "You can either love me or leave me." Better is the adage of, "Accept me for who I am." Such doctrines that we have chosen for our lives have been at our own detriment. There is simply no room for growth in forcing people to accept you for who you are. How can you grow if you are accepted at the very state you are in? Why would you declare such limits for yourself?

These thinking patterns produce mass complacency. We soon find that our lives are stagnant and we wonder why things are the way that they are. Well, it is because we remain who we are. It is simple math and it is time we consider adding this all up. It has never been cool, from where I sit, to refuse challenges that can make us greater, stronger and wiser. A challenge to give up smoking, drinking, overeating or any bad habits is a challenge worth accepting. Sure it seems big, but this is a part of the adjustment phase. Think of it this way: If you are a chain smoker and now challenged from your doctor to give it up to avoid lung cancer, the true essence is found in now having to find something more to do with your time. Your time is connected to the many cigarettes you puff on each day. The problem is deeply rooted in what fostered the habit in the first place. The newness of your life is found in getting to the root of what brought this on as a problem.

I have heard of so many stories where people learned of a cancerous state then immediately gave up the deadly habit itself. This has led me to believe in the power of our will and ability as human beings. What is present upon receiving news of a potential death from cancer is present when hearing of the statistics of your likelihood to inherit the disease. Somehow, 100% of smokers consider themselves as part of that small 10% who are said to not contract lung cancer. They figure that "it won't happen to me." Yet, when it does, there are many who testify to their awesome ability, via a tenacious human spirit, to immediately break the habit. Perhaps this is connected to the will to live and an awesome ability to change.

It is my position that, beyond smokers, each of us remains challenged almost daily in areas that make and break us. We have comfortably uninvited these challenges because of our personally constructed comfort zones, and then we complain of our predicaments. We cannot have it both ways. We must accept the challenge as merely an adjustment to our lives. It changes us and grows us. Truly, we are not responsible for some of the things that have led us to the places we are in, yet we are responsible for getting to where we need to be. I often say that we cannot, as a society, blame the victim; yet the victim is not blameless. The victims in my instructional context are the many Black folk who have been victimized as Americans, tortured because of their texture and criticized because of their color. Our victim status is short-lived when we accept and adjust to not being blameless.

Blameless victims are those that refuse responsibility of their own actions. They are not accountable and lean on being victims rather than moving toward victory. One of the greatest challenges in life is found in making necessary adjustments in our lives. We must be accountable. We must show responsibility in changing our lives. The challenge for us all is found in the adjustment of changing. In the end, it works for us in great ways. To not change that which is detrimental to our development is to accept what is simply not working for us. We must challenge what is before us and thus change that which is within us.

CLIMB THE MOUNTAIN

Who said it would be easy anyway? For years you have held onto the pain, suffering in silence, allowing the pain of your past to stain your present and stunt your growth for a better future. So many are just like you in that life's unfortunate circumstances keep them bound. I suggest to you, climb the mountain! Step on the hills of fear and forgive yourself. Climb the mountain of faith and forward move. I liken our lives to a computer where we tend to store the problems of our lives in files. We place them away in the computer's memory while refusing to trash them completely. The files remain stored away as we continue coping with life as opposed to living the fullness of our lives.

The beauty of life is found in our ability to overcome. We all love a story where adversity is overthrown with a will to live and a power to win. Our moment of overcoming awaits us. To begin, we must open the file we stored so long ago. What do I mean? Well, you may have been molested, abused, beaten, cursed, attacked, adopted, lost, given away, thrown out, shut out, betrayed, raped, rejected, neglected, unprotected or nearly murdered. Perhaps, it was your incarcerated father or your drug-addicted mother that touched you inappropriately, and now you do not want anyone touching you at all. As for the culprit in your life, you gave him authority unknowingly and began to participate willingly. Incest became a relationship and daddy became 'your man.' Now these files represent the pain of your past and the virus in the system of your adult life. It keeps you bound. You want to deal with it but who do you tell? How do you tell it? One of the greatest tricks of the enemy is found in you believing that you are alone. You are not, nor are you the first to have to endure such tragedy. The truth is you have everything you need to forgive and release and there is no better time than now.

Unfortunately, we as a community of people reject the blessing of counseling. I like calling it "couch time." We have been conditioned to thinking that only "crazy" people see counselors, or shrinks, as we like to say. The truth is counselors, like attorneys and doctors, are experts in the area of psychological healing. As we consult attorneys as specialists of law, we should also consult counselors as specialists in healing our minds and hearts. As a people, we have bought into these myths at our own detriment. Do you not want deliverance? Sure, God can heal you. It is indeed what He does daily with so many of us. However, He has also been known to satisfy our requests for blessings through the mechanisms of His children. I believe with all of my being that, be it counselors or teachers, God is able to use each of these for our growth and development.

In an attempt to truly clean the memory of our life computers, we need help. For too long we have held onto spirits that encourage us not to forgive. We are bitter, thus we are not better. We sit and wonder why our lives are in turmoil and we have actually decided to hate those who hurt us, not realizing that this actually stifles our own development. Truly, the things I am mentioning for your ultimate survival and peace are not easy, yet they are doable. We are more times than none all of who we are because of the unresolved mess in our lives. If we are completely honest, we can notice in our own behaviors and attitudes the very things we do not like in others. You may abuse women because you saw your dad do the same thing. You may accept abuse because you saw mom do this. You drink, curse, smoke and remain promiscuous because it was your learning curve growing up. In the end, you do not really like who you have become yet you refuse to access this file and drag it to the trash. It is who you are, or is it?

I have stopped by in this essay to yet again remind you of God's grace. Falling short of God's glory does not have to permanently remove you from your divine destiny. Climb the mountain! You have some work to do and you can do it by first desiring to abort those things that keep you bound — climb the mountain! You are called to do great things and your past has passed yet your future is for you — climb the mountain.

What do I mean in climbing the mountain? Well, the time has come for you to reach the top in your life by getting to the bottom of your issues. It will take work; it's one step at a time, but you must climb. You do not have to build the mountain; you just have to climb it to your successful place. One step and one day at a time, begin to unravel your new and next level with God. Open those files, receive counseling and help in processing the pain of your life. Pray over the pain you are being delivered from and trash it. Delete it forever and let's rebuild a new anti-virus system of life that cooperates with God's healing and destiny in your life. Climb the mountain!

WHY NOT AFRICA?

There seems to be a consistent pattern in our communities on how we view the continent of Africa. Admittedly even I was, as Malcolm X would say, "bamboozled and led astray." I recall the many times growing up in my neighborhood where we would "play the dozens" or as we said, signify. There were a few things that were intolerable in those moments though and it was the limitation placed on signifying when it came to "your momma" jokes. It's interesting in looking back how the larger insult was the signifying moment we all, at some point, shared in calling someone an "African booty scratcher." Prompting the most laughter, it seemed as if this joke never got old. Yet it has to be the most ignorant component of those signifying moments. What was so funny about this, I now ask? Where did this emerge from and why did we continue such in conversation?

For years we have learned that Africa is a place where certain animals, resembling us as Black folk, swing from trees. We have been taught that Africa is a place where people actually eat other people. The imagery that we receive early on in our lives relative to Africa has proved extremely detrimental throughout our lives. Moreover, this stigma of being barbaric and animalistic damages our mindsets even here in America. How we see ourselves is intricately connected to the limitations we have on ourselves. Our inability to be strong and mighty is hazardously interwoven with weak teachings regarding who we allegedly are. At best, this dangerous religion is "Confused-ianity" and its largest congregation is that of our communities.

While some might argue against these heightened levels of confusion among us, I declare that it is quite obvious when one enters our communities. The character of our neighbors best defines the character of our neighborhoods. We litter in our communities because we have littered minds. The widespread existence of vacant lots has helped produce our vacant thinking. What do we critically question? Why do we just accept emptiness? The vacancy of our attacks against such madness has led us to just accepting things as if we cannot change these things. Did Harriet Tubman accept slavery? Did Rev. Dr. Martin Luther King, Jr. accept segregation? Did Jesus accept an unrighteous world? We are defined daily by what it is we accept. And, oddly, our acceptance of such mess is connected to the messages we continually receive that suggest we are less than, weaker than and even dumber than. Well, who are we weaker and dumber than? Are we truly less than any others?

Recently, CNN hired Margaret Beale Spencer, a leading researcher in the field of child development, to conduct a pilot study on race and how it's viewed among White and Black children. Nearly seventy years after the landmark Doll Test conducted by psychologists Kenneth and Mamie Clark in the 1940's, this similar study garnered some of the same alarming results.

A White child looks at a picture of a Black child and says she's bad because she's Black. A Black child says adults prefer a White child because of their lighter skin tone. Decades after the Civil Rights Movement, we continue to witness unchanged attitudes in the face of a so-called changed environment. As startling evidence continually suggests the existence of racial tenets in our society, far too many still downplay their effects on Black folk in particular.

Seldom have we learned of the genius of African culture that erected pyramids and the land that gave the world diamonds, gold and other valuable minerals. As the civilization capital of the world, this great continent currently represents nearly 15% of the world's human population with recent figures topping 1,000,000,000 people. Ironically, the Chinese are the fastest growing business group in Africa today. As Black folk continue to joke about and despise their own cultural connection to Africa, it is the very place other cultures are benefiting from and growing their business agendas in today. And as they seek to purchase property, build and develop in Africa, we are bombarded here in America with limiting and degrading imagery that tears down our potential.

Why not Africa? Why not greatness? Why not?

This is a globally connected world. Mark Zuckerberg, co-founder of Facebook has a growing consumer base of 500 million people. His success is intricately connected to access. His brilliant mind was fostered early on in his life as he had access to computers as a child, which debatably contributed to his informed mind and creative thinking. Mr. Zuckerberg's brilliance is admirable and my assessment does not take away from such. It is important to highlight, however, what happens in communities where access is limited and minds are trained to be limiting. Many Black folk and poorer Americans by and large obtained computers in their households just within the last decade or so. As the youngest billionaire, Mr. Zuckerberg and his current success is indeed exemplary of his genius and work ethic. However, we must acknowledge how access privileged him to be who he is today. He attended Harvard University. What happens when such access is not an option? What can we learn from Mr. Zuckerberg's life chances and choices?

Blackademically Speaking, it is time we develop a new social network, which speaks personally to our crisis. It is time that we alter our desires. So much of what we desire is connected to what we have, in our ignorance, been trained to admire. If what we desire is not aligned with what we truly deserve as royalty, then the results are what we have before us. We must establish a new network, posting courage, character and conviction on our wall for clarity. We must only accept education and actualization as our new friends. It is not enough to understand the problems of the day; it is now time to best educate ourselves while properly preparing ourselves for the future. It is necessary to actualize a global plan educationally to best effect change culturally. ***Why not Africa?***

?-? LOL

Just months before my daddy made his transition, I found myself in a hilarious conversation with one of my good friends. While visiting with her and her mom, I explained to them how my dad was becoming more engaged technologically. After purchasing a Blackberry device, his usage of e-mails and text messages increased. Considering this, I soon influenced him to adopt the symbol "LOL" via some of my messages. In my conversation with them, I joked with how I initially told him it meant "lots of love" and how I failed to share its most utilized form as a set phrase meaning "laughing out loud."

In sharing this most amusing story, I declared that I would have to soon clarify this point to my dad as he had made a habit of signing each of his text messages with an "LOL" before his name. Many would soon question his constant signature of "laughing out loud," especially in messages that were serious in nature. Amazingly, my friend and her mom suggested that I keep things as they were with Daddy, allowing him to do his own thing. Well, my daddy never received the most popular meaning of LOL. Instead, he departed us with the only meaning I shared with him —"lots of love."

On July 3, 2010, I eulogized my daddy through the sermon's theme, "What's new in you?" It is indeed amazing to know God as the powerful deity that He is, as it was His strength that carried me through such a task. On that day, I challenged all to evaluate their lives in the spirit of newness. It was newness that my dad experienced as he finished his human cycle of life, and I know that it is newness that you, the reader, shall embark upon for change.

Champions Break Chains is written with "lots of love." It is a God-inspired work that challenges you. It is written as a charge for you to do the work to change what is in you. It is in the spirit of our strong ancestry that we carry out the work necessary in breaking the chains. This book was written to not only incite a pleasurable reading encounter but also to ignite a memorable action experience. So, it is here that I challenge you to do something about your hyphen-lived reality. It is here that I ask you to choose life as a champion beyond the chains. We need not see the statistics plaguing our communities as the end results for our lives. In fact, it is the different results in our lives that will alter the statistics. It is here that I invite you to a new way of living and thinking. Thus, it is this framework of principles and tenets which I supply you with in becoming a CHAMPION:

> **Conviction** - As you challenge yourself to be better, greater, wiser, and stronger, make up your mind that you will not waver. Stop settling for things because of fear. Move in faith and be convicted!

> **Honesty** - Tell the truth! Live the truth and do not distort the truth! Dishonesty destroys even the best relationships. Live honestly and choose honesty!

> **Attitude** - Insist on a positive attitude! Stop being bitter and get better! Change your perspective on things and kill the negative attitude! Know this: it is not the people

in your environment causing your bad days; it's your INvironment (what's already IN you) that's causing your sad ways. Change your attitude!

Mentor - Find a mentor and choose to mentor someone as well. Key point: if you haven't broken your personal chains, and you aren't living as a champion, then don't try to mentor anyone. Put a strong emphasis on getting a mentor first!

Pedagogy - Just because a teacher loves teaching math, this does not mean that the teacher will effectively teach math to all students, particularly to "Mike-Mike." And just because you don't know what pedagogy means, it does not mean you are not being affected by it daily. Demand that teachers practice a culturally relevant pedagogy. It is simply not enough to teach the subject matter. Pedagogy is an art, a method for teaching that incorporates what really matters which is the student understanding the subject. Pedagogy, pedagogy, pedagogy!

Integrity - Stop living life on layaway. Purchase outright those things that will enhance your character wardrobe, i.e., virtue, dignity and integrity. Cancel your layaway plan of instability and foolishness. Why continue to make payments on such? Stand tall and stand strong! Have virtue! Be dignified! And live with Integrity!

Obedience - Listen to your parents! You're never too old to do this. If your parents raised you, and put up with you, are they not worthy of your attention when they want to tell you a few things? And if God created our parents, is He not worthy of our obedience? All children are charged to obey their parents. All of God's children should obey God.

Never Again - This two-word principle in this Champion framework is far better than the two words "it's over." All too often we refer to slavery being over as opposed to saying "Never Again." Sure, life on the plantation is over, but remnants remain. Failing to teach our children about slavery is as futile as declaring "it's over." We must teach our children about this evil act of humanity, just as we must insist, "Never Again!"

Spiritual - In a world that chooses fast cars over fast cures, we need people that are Spiritual. In 1900, the three leading causes of death in the U.S. were pneumonia, tuberculosis (TB), and diarrhea. Advances in public health, medicine and research helped alter this human devastation. Can you imagine not having a treatment plan or cure for your diarrhea? Spiritual people care about all people; thus, we need more spiritual leadership. We need spirit-led family units. Call an old friend; forgive a family member. Trust me, now is a good time to grow up! One day you will grow old and discover what matters most. Get to know your grandparents and elders in your family. Call them and treat them to lunch. Live by those priceless adages such as, "Treat people how you want to be treated....what goes around comes around...and it takes a village to raise a child." I now know that if "it takes a village to raise a child" then it takes an intelligent and spiritually sound village to teach one. Social networking sites cannot properly raise our children. Nothing compares to the development gained from personally networking with your family. Watch how you spend your time and watch whom you spend your time with as well. Develop lasting relationships and remember, "a chain is only as strong as its weakest link." Choose to be strong — Choose to be Spiritual!

Blackademically Speaking encourages the change in you! If 70% of health care costs are lifestyle related then should we champion health care reform or lifestyle reform? It is time to change our thinking and our doing; it is time to change our lives! We are not good enough and there's so much more to our lives.

As Americans continue to debate within a two-party political system, we're lagging the world educationally. Overwhelmingly, India, China and other countries send their students here for their college degrees. Taking education very seriously, these foreign students dominate collegiate classrooms. Meanwhile, in stark contrast, I seldom witness such preparation amongst students raised in our culture. Do we take pride in sending our children to China for their four-year degrees? Proper preparation for such realities involves learning languages, an openness to global travel and an understanding of culture beyond America.

Stuck in our arrogant ignorance, other countries create the very video games our children waste so much time playing. It is the video gaming industry that best exposes the limiting globally-academic competition our culture can muster. Continually, we seek to dominate when playing video games against others throughout the world. Nevertheless, as they sell us the product, they continually dominate us in the science and math that makes international gaming possible.

Champions Break Chains acknowledges the Champion in you. It is time to champion winning beyond PS3™ and Wii. It is time to rise as champions in the Spirit of Love. It is time for motivation and proper education. As my daddy said regarding my weekly words of motivation:

> "To become who we aspire to be is eloquently transcribed in your messages. I have always thought the mind must be clean to think clearly. Thank you for proving that thought. LOL Dad"

It is my prayer that the messages in this book brings out the best of your hyphen experience. I pray that you eloquently live in love and with "lots" of it.

Break the chains!

- NARRATIVES -

◇◇

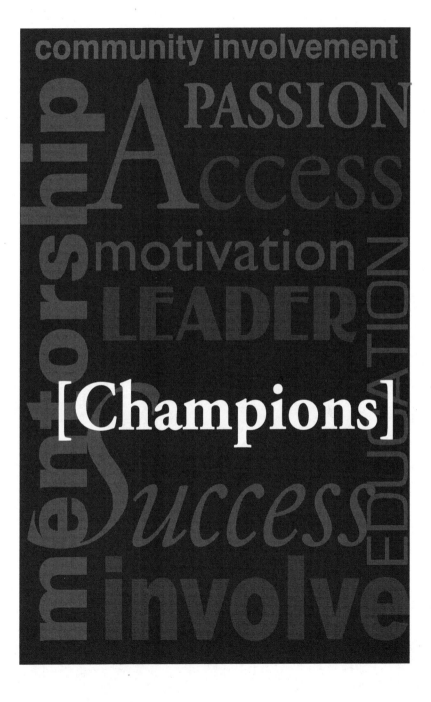

Savitri Boodram, 25
Born in Urbana, IL
Business Administration, B.S. Depaul University
Masters of Business Administration (MBA) University of Illinois @ Urbana-Champaign
Occupation: Entrepreneur

As a young woman of color, any color, mentorship provides a type of motivation not found in the home, or in the school system, but found only in the admiration and closeness that you develop with a person of success. Seeing someone successful, motivating and leading are qualities for which one can speak about but only truly benefits from seeing and experiencing. I have known Chandra Gill since I was just entering high school. Meeting her at such a critical time in my life truly shaped my future in countless ways. Not only through my relationship with Chandra was I introduced to the strong characteristics of leadership and motivation in action but I was introduced to community involvement, mentorship, educational access, and campus initiatives. Throughout high school my relationship with Chandra allowed me to attend college visits, recognize the importance of higher education decisions and encourage those around me to recognize it too. This relationship also allowed me to attend leadership events and conventions while eventually leading and organizing leadership activities for others. In completing my MBA degree I knew that my success was attributed to my ability to recognize the importance of education and, thanks to Chan, identify a path that would lead me.

Most importantly I gained an invaluable friendship with someone of great character, someone who even on the darkest days, some of which I witnessed firsthand, continued to have a resolve that only the strongest and most grounded women possess. Not only do I contribute some of my most important academic successes to Chandra but I also recognize that I was not the only one influenced in this way. She truly started an ever-growing ripple effect that will affect my generation, this generation, and many to come. Her true contributions to so many communities can never truly be known, and that I appreciate the most.

One funny moment that I want to leave you with is, on a college tour to Atlanta, Georgia, myself, and three peers were in our hotel room excited about our Atlanta arrival and the college tours the next day. All of a sudden Chandra runs through the hotel room door and jumps on the first bed, screaming "ATL, ATL, ATL!" We laughed for days at her and the fact that she was just as excited as we were!

Sharial Howard, 29
Born in Hazlehurst, MS
Speech Communication, B.A. University of Illinois @ Urbana-Champaign
Occupation: Paralegal, Walgreens Company

I met Dr. Chandra Nicole Gill my sophomore year in high school. I was on my way to a tutoring session in Lincoln Hall at the University of Illinois at Urbana-Champaign. As I walked through the hallway of Lincoln Hall, Chandra asked, "Do you practice abstinence?" Although I was a virgin, I didn't respond because I couldn't understand why she would ask me, that question. From that day on, Chandra has served as my mentor and friend. Her bold personality, coupled with her passion for serving others are merely two characteristics that I admire. In my opinion, a mentor is one who sacrifices their time and effort for someone else. More specifically, a mentor is one who teaches, serves as a role model and helps others achieve their goals. Chandra always told me that there are those who make things happen, watch what happens, or wonder what happened. Chandra is definitely the type of mentor that makes things happen. She took me under her wings and treated me as if she had known me her whole life. From tutoring me, assisting me with my personal statement for the admittance into the University of Illinois at Urbana-Champaign, to helping me become the intelligent Black woman I am today, I can truly attest to the fact that Chandra has been there for me from the moment we met. Chandra has taught me some valuable lessons and she has definitely sacrificed her time for me. Because of the time she sacrificed, I was admitted into the University of Illinois at Urbana-Champaign and graduated.

Erica A. Walker, 31

Born in Chicago, IL

Advertising, B.S. University of Illinois at Urbana-Campaign

Occupation: Customer Service Manager & SAP Systems Analyst

I first met Chandra as a freshman on the University of Illinois Campus back in 1997. If memory serves me correctly, she was passing out flyers to publicize the Back to School Blast, which was a community service project organized by the women of Delta Sigma Theta Sorority, Inc. I admit, what first drew me to Chandra was her membership in the very organization I dreamed of joining. Little did I know that God would allow our relationship to blossom into one of mentor/mentee, sisters in Delta and then eventually friends. The more I got to know Chandra, the more I got to learn about the type of woman I wanted to be and about how important it was to give back to the communities you live in as well as those you're educated in. I can recall a time where we discussed our upbringing and our faith in God while sitting in Chandra's car. As the conversation intensified, I began to cry while I expressed my insecurities, fears, future plans for my life and about giving up my dream of being a Delta. Chandra then gave me some of the best advice that I incorporate in my life to this day. She told me that I was a strong young woman with a good heart who needed to always believe in myself. She reminded me of the many obstacles I had already overcome to get to U of I and how I had an inner strength to succeed against all odds that should never be forgotten. She always gave me her most honest opinion in a constructive way with a few scriptures to back it up. Those that know Chandra know that she always has a scripture and likes to incorporate God in everything and in every lesson. I never wanted to admit it then, but somehow her scriptures and advice always seem to make me feel better and encouraged me to press forward with my head always held high.

Chandra has always been a source of light and inspiration to those around her. You may not agree with everything she says but you come to respect her for speaking her mind and for staying true to herself. I learned the true definition of giving back with an open heart from Chandra and somehow volunteering always made whatever I was going through seem easier to tackle. Today I am a Manager and Analyst for one of the countries largest steel companies. I attained my position and status there, through hard work, dedication, and in being professional. I am known amongst my co-workers as one who's outspoken and serious about maintaing my integrity. I am involved with my company's community outreach programs, making sure that they support local community projects as well as global initiatives. No matter where my life will lead me, the guidance Chandra provided me will always play a major role in what I do, how I do it, and where I end up. I'll still march to my own drum and stay true to my heart but I will never forget my mentor, my sister in Delta, and my friend, Dr. Chandra Gill.

India Boodram, 25
Born In Urbana, IL
Business Administration, B.S. Depaul University
Masters of Business Administration (MBA) University of Illinois @ Urbana-Champaign
Occupation: Entrepreneur

Chan and I began our relationship over a decade ago when she arrived
at my high school to tell us about a great program sponsored by Delta
Sigma Theta Sorority, Inc. This youth centered program encouraged
young minority women to become involved in their community. Over
the years I have found a true friend and mentor in Chandra Gill. She
truly speaks to what a strong woman and mentor is. She is a daily
encouragement in my life and she teaches me, repeatedly, the value in
never giving up and always keeping hope and faith alive. Thanks to Chan
I have accomplished more in my life than I thought possible. While I
know she can't be with me every step of the way, she has instilled in me
the tools that I need to achieve and be successful. For me, this is what
makes her a great mentor.

I remember the day of the incident at our school. It was one of the
longest days of my life. We left the school and headed to the hospital after
the ambulance left. They didn't allow anyone to ride with her so we waited
for updates until we reached the emergency room. When we arrived, the
waiting room was full of people-there for Chan. In waiting word regarding
Chandra's condition, we all prayed. As soon as we finished praying, we
were told she was arrested from her hospital bed and taken out of the back
door. That night I'm not sure anyone slept and as soon as the morning
came we all went to the jailhouse to demand for her release. There were
hundreds of people protesting. It was amazing to see how many lives Chan

touched. We waited there until she was released. As she exited the jail, everyone cheered and screamed. I was in tears by then and I remember running to hug her. I think all of us were still in shock about the whole ordeal. Yet we remained close. In fact she was supported the entire trial period and even after Chan's pardon was received.

Victoria Whiteside, 25
Born in Urbana, IL
Public Health, B.S. University of Illinois @ Urbana-Champaign;
Public Health, MPH University of Illinois @ Springfield
Occupation: Medicaid Consultant

My name is Victoria Whiteside however Dr. Chandra Gill calls me "Little Bit." I first met Chandra when she came to my high school for Del-Teens, a high school mentoring program under Delta Sigma Theta Sorority, Inc. At that time I didn't know much about the group, but I knew they hung out with college women so I applied and was selected. I can remember talking to Chandra and thinking, "she is so smart and well spoken, one day I will be like her." I was the stereotypical black student. I had grown up in Champaign-Urbana, in a low-income, single parent household. I was smart but had no real direction. During the first year in Del-Teens Chandra took us on a college tour. I had never really been out of Champaign, but on that tour I saw so many black students going to college for the first time. It really made believe that I could go to college too. Over the years Del-Teens and more specifically Chan was an important driving force in me deciding that I would go to college. Chandra always spoke with such conviction of her beliefs in me and that meant the world to me. She instilled in me the importance of community service and education. After graduating from high school I went to the University of Illinois and became the Community Service chair for Central Black Student Union and a mentor at the Boys and Girls Club. My most memorable moment of Chandra was her pinning me at our Sorority's induction ceremony, in the very Chapter she had mentored me as a teen. I continue my community service through various avenues both privately and through Delta Sigma Theta Sorority, Inc. Throughout my college days and still today, Chandra has always been there to support me not only as a mentor but as a friend. Today I am a first generation college student and currently working on a Masters in Public Health. I am a consultant for Medicaid and I mentor 8th graders, locally.

Geovonda Anai Stoner, 25
Born in Decatur, IL
Occupation: Mental Health Tech

I met Chandra when I was 14 years old when I attended my first Delteens meeting-an organization sponsored by Delta Sigma Theta Incorporated. It is for African-American high school aged girls, focusing on education and community service. The meeting was led by Chandra. I remember the first day I met Chan at the foreign language building on the University of Illinois campus I was so amazed by the way she conducted herself in such a professional manner and the way she worded things so intelligently. I remember thinking wow she is so intelligent and at times even being intimidated by her sophistication. I didn't know much about Chan at that time but I couldn't help but think I want to be like her.

Chandra has definitely helped shape me in becoming the person I am today (and in more ways than one). I can thank her for having a voice about things I feel strongly about, taking initiative in my community and striving to be a better person each day. I am currently a big sister in Big Brother Big Sister Organization because I recognize the importance of giving back and being active in a person's life. I know the significance it can have on a young girl growing up to have a person that she can confide in and help lead her down a positive road because Chandra was that for me. Being a mentor now I didn't realize the amount of responsibility you take on in this role. In thinking back, Chandra had to have been stressed because she took on that role for so many. From the day I first met Chan I have looked up to her and have enjoyed listening to her lectures, engaging in conversations and discussions. Going into some conversations with Chan I used to think we're going to be talking for a while because Chandra has a way of keeping you engaged on a topic. Although the discussions were long I couldn't wait to hear the motivation behind her theory or point. Chandra always made me feel like there is nothing I couldn't accomplish. Chandra has influenced me to keep the faith even when things are going bad. My friends and I, all of whom Chandra advised, had a running joke when we would find ourselves in bad situations; "what would Chandra do" was our question, because she was so positive.

I remember a minor situation that took place in my sophomore year with my biology teacher questioning my faith. She made comments about my religion stating, "we give God too much credit." She said "when you sit in a chair you don't put faith in God that the chair will hold you up but you hope that the creator of the chair built the chair well." Basically saying Life is not about faith in God it is about science and hope. I remember being upset about her putting down my God and the first person I could think of was Chandra, and as always she was there. That following day Chan was there to test the knowledge of my teacher. When she was done I remember my teacher asking her for her number and wanting to talk more in depth about Chan's viewpoint. That situation empowered me all the more and I remember thinking, "how does she do it?"

Our highlighted, yet sad moment came when we asked Chandra to attend a basketball game our junior year; it was a game you just couldn't miss. We played against our rivalry team. Chandra of course willingly honored our request and was right there, cheering with us. What was a great night turned into a night we will never forget. Still we wish it never had happened. While Chandra's faith was obviously tested, she grew stronger. I remember feeling at one point that it was my entire fault. I began to think, if I hadn't asked her to be there this would not have happened. I apologized to Chandra and I remember her saying "what did you do, you did nothing wrong I was there because I wanted to be there." I remember feeling so much better in hearing those words. Chan soon thereafter said, "God won't put more on us than we can bear." I remember thinking "only Chan can take something like this and make it positive, allowing her faith to guide her in the direction God had planned for her." Chandra is a dynamic person, mentor and advisor! I have come in contact with several people but I can honestly say I haven't met a person close to Chan. She is a blessing from God to all that she has made contact with. Chandra is inspirational, intelligent, funny, loving and humble. The most admirable part of Chan is that throughout everything, God is first in her life. There is no obstacle to BIG for her to overcome. I am blessed to have had the opportunity to have Chandra in my life. In Delteens we always opened our meetings with a quote because Chan taught us that a lot can be said through a quote, so what better way to end this than by a quote…

… To the world you may be one person, but to one person you maybe the world

Chan, you deserve all the BLESSINGS that come your way. You are more than a mentor and advisor to me. I can't thank you enough for the positive impact you have had on my life! I love you!

Shonta Connolly, 28
Born in Chicago, IL
Consumer Textile Marketing, B.S. University of Illinois @ Urbana-Champaign
Occupation: Managed Services, National Account Manager

One of my top goals entering college was to become more independent, to learn to stand on my own, making good decisions. I thought that I could do this alone, and that asking for help and looking to someone for guidance was being dependent on them. Well, I quickly found out I was mistaken.

When I met Chandra, she naturally embraced my friendship and *started* helping me. I learn the most from seeing things in action. Chandra was most influential in my life just by letting me be around her, watching how she interacted with others, how she analyzed situations, how she so eloquently and professionally spoke and gave encouragement.

In some instances I felt like a mooch, in that I kept taking and not giving her anything in return. I would use her when I was feeling down about my grades, and she would lift me up. I would use her when I didn't know how to respond to a situation brought before me, and she would walk me through it. I would listen to her encouraging words and leave feeling like I could conquer the world. I recall a situation in particular when some friends visited me on campus. I saw Chandra at a local gas station. I audaciously asked her to speak to my friends, to encourage them. Still today, they reference Chandra, asking how she's doing. It amazes me that they still remember the conversation and the lessons they received. What I imagined would be a five minute encounter, considering it was at a gas station, lasted just over an hour. Just recently, another friend referenced that moment. I thought to myself, how could one person talk to a group of people for just an hour and leave a lasting 10 plus year impression on them?

What I loved most about Chandra is that she's natural. She did nothing outside of her character, that day. I had nothing to offer her. She wasn't using me to advance her in any way in her life. She was just being true to who she was and being a great friend and mentor. This might sound like nothing extraordinary for you, but it was more than I ever needed.

You would think that with me being an "adult," that I would be self-sustained where I didn't need her guidance or encouragement. But it's more now than before. And although we only speak once every three to four months, we can never be on a call shorter than an hour or so. We would walk through every point in my life and she would give me feedback, encouragement, referrals or prayer. She's there to just listen too.

In my eyes she is an unbelievable woman with talents beyond compare. Unfortunately I still feel like a mooch, but at least I admit it!

Many girls at our school wanted to be in sororities. One in particular was Delta Sigma Theta, Inc. And many girls on campus knew that Chandra held a high rank within DST. Chandra was also co-founder of an organization called Project: Youth. In which many girls joined just to get close to her, selfishly so that they could become a member.

Well, one day Chandra pulled me to the side, and asked me my intentions of being in Project: Youth. She wanted to know if I was only trying to build a relationship with her, due to me wanting to be a member. That was a defining moment, as I knew that Chandra was very serious about Project: Youth and our mission of helping underprivileged students. I was a part of Project: Youth solely because I liked the mission of the organization. Additionally as her mentee, I truly thought she was phenomenal. That night, I felt as if Chandra was qualifying my intentions and from that moment she was able to trust me and accept me as her mentee and our relationship grew further than I ever could have imagined.

It's an ongoing joke, between Chandra and I, how I take that of what Chandra says when speaking. I try to reinvent it as if I said it, especially statistics, but it doesn't seem to have the same effect; yet it is still powerful. I love that according to "Friends Law" friends cannot sue other friends for plagiarism, for I would owe Chandra a lot of money! I thank her for her words over the years that not only helped me in my life, but too helped so many others. Truly, I used those same words of encouragement to help lift give confidence to those around me.

Crystal T. Lee, 25

Born in Chicago, IL

Psychology / Sociology / Anthropology, B.A. Fisk University

Technology Management and Homeland Security Management, M.S.

Occupation: Intelligence Analyst for the Federal Government

Chandra has had a MAJOR influence on my life in several areas. Chandra's life is a living testimony of God's love, mercy, and favor. When I think of Chandra, I immediately think of a woman of virtue, perseverance, tenacity, patience, wisdom, and strength. Chandra encourages me to strive for the best, to face every obstacle, trial, and test with the full armor of God, and to trust God with everything, even if I cannot trace him. She's taught me to believe in myself no matter what people and statistics may say about young African American women living in America.

During Fall (2005) semester of my undergraduate studies, I was told that as a Ronald McNair scholar it was required that I complete an internship during Summer (2006). One of my professors told me about an internship program with a federal government agency whose mission aligned with my research interest. She informed me that the agency picks one person from each of their 56 offices located throughout the United States. I decided to go to the website to conduct further research. I found out that it was a 12 week paid internship in Washington DC and I met all of the requirements. The only problem was that the application was due in 48 hours. I had to have one of my professors write a recommendation, personal statement, college transcripts, criminal background check, credit check, and health examination. As you can see the application process was very rigorous.

I remember thinking to myself, "Crystal, do you honestly think you are going to be selected for this internship? The deadline is in 48 hours!" I remember praying about the situation and God spoke to me and told me to move forward with the application and to call Chandra for help. I knew that Chandra was a BUSY lady; however, she always told me that she would make time for me. I called her thinking to myself, "I wonder if she's busy? Will she have time to talk to me? She's going to say "Crystal why did you wait to the last minute." I thought of a million things she could have said. I was wrong.

Chandra answered the phone and my heart dropped. I asked her if she was busy. She told me that she was in the car driving to Champaign, IL and had time to talk to me. I told her all about the internship and asked her to help me with my personal statement. She answered, "Yes." I asked her would she have time to discuss the personal statement, since she was on the road. She told me that we could write the statement together while she was driving. She reiterated that the application was due in now (24 Hours) and we needed to get things done quickly.

We began to discuss and write the personal statement over the phone. We did not get off of the phone until the statement was complete. I was able to email her a draft of the statement for review before she made it to Champaign, IL. The personal statement was awesome! I read it over and over again. She helped me organize my thoughts, highlight my educational achievements, and future career objectives in a clear and concise format. Chandra is a gifted writer. My personal statement read like a story. I could not wait to mail my application to the local office, which was in Memphis, TN. Approximately three days later, the executive manager of the Memphis office called me personally to tell me she reviewed my application and was impressed. I was the last application the office received before the deadline. She informed me that an individual from the agency would be at my university the next day. She wanted me to meet him. Approximately 3 months later, I received a letter offering me the internship for Summer 2006. I called Chandra and told her thank you for helping me at the last minute and told her that all of our hard work paid off. I was offered the internship and was selected to represent the state of Tennessee in the agency's honors internship program.

I thank God for blessing me with Chandra. She's not only my mentor; she's my big sister, my friend, and my sister in Christ. I can always depend on Chandra to be there through good times and difficult times. I currently work for the organization I interned for in 2006.

I've known Chandra since I was a little girl in diapers. She likes to tell people that whenever she has the opportunity. Chandra and my sister (Joy) grew up together on the south side of Chicago, IL. When I was in elementary school I did not want to be around Chandra because she always challenged me. I will NEVER forget how I would go out with her and Joy and she would always ask me to solve math problems or ask me a black history related question. Sometimes I would know the answer and other times I had no clue. I never told her this...I used to study multiplication and black history facts because of her. I used to ask Joy when Chandra was coming around so that I could prepare myself to talk to her. She is the first woman I met that actually challenged me to learn more. As a little child, I always wanted to develop a personal relationship with her. I just did not know how to do it.

Chandra was the first person from my neighborhood to go to college. I never had any aspirations to go to school till I witnessed her go away to school and achieve multiple degrees. I remember thinking to myself, "if Chandra can do it, I know I can do it." I guess Chandra felt the same way.

During my senior year of high school my mother's breast cancer spread to her lungs. She became very ill and died December 7, 2002. Chandra was there for me every step of the way. After you experience a death in your family many people say, "if you need me please let me know and I will be there." Chandra told me those very words and she was there for me every step of the way. She knew it was time for me to prepare for college. Chandra helped me research schools, scholarships, and helped write my personal statement for undergraduate applications. After I went away to school she never stopped being there for me. Chandra used to send me $25 dollars ever month. She never knew how much that meant to me. Some months I did not have money for food. She also helped me purchase my books for school.

Chandra started off as my sister's friend. She later became my mentor, now she's my mentor, friend, and third big sister. I can talk to Chandra about religion, politics, school, work, relationships, love, marriage, finances, children, and more. Chandra will always hold a special place in my heart. I attribute many of my accomplishments to her. Thanks for being an example of what it means to be God's servant. You continue to serve God by helping others. I cannot wait to witness the awesome things God has in store for Chandra.

Now, I am a mentor. God has blessed me with many opportunities and blessings in life. It is my duty to share my testimony to help others who think that they cannot make it. It is my duty to be a light in dark places. It is my duty to be a servant leader and help others by meeting them where they are in life. My relationship with Chandra encourages me to reach out and help others. She's never stopped serving her community throughout her life. She makes it a priority to selflessly serve others. Many people who go away to college and earn advance degrees never return back to their childhood communities to help out. I've watched Chandra do the opposite for many years and it encourages me to help those who are in need where I am. I dedicate time to mentor others every week. I look forward to serving others each and every day. I am here today because of all the sacrifices others have made to encourage me.

Dr. Tyra J. Manso, 30
Born in Chicago, IL
Chemistry, B.S. University of Illinois @ Urbana-Champaign
D.D.S. University of Michigan School of Dentistry
Pediatric Dental Residency Lutheran Medical Central-Brooklyn NY
Occupation: Pediatric Dentist

I was born and raised in Chicago and attended Lindblom Technical High School. As a result of Project: Youth coming to my high school to encourage students to go to college I applied to the University of Illinois. I had good grades in high school and was involved in extra curricular activities but I had no idea how to go about applying or picking a school since I was the first in my family to go to college. In fact, U of I was the only college I even applied to. I remember always wanting to be a dentist even when I was young so I went to the university planning to major in Chemistry. I remember my second semester came and I was stressed about how I was going to afford to stay at the university. My mother was working two jobs and raising my brother back at home. I had to call and tell her how much it would cost to continue school and how much I needed for books and lab fees. I remember walking around campus and just being thankful. I knew that God was responsible for me being there on campus and he wouldn't let me fail.

I was walking and praying asking God to show me how I was going to make it. A young woman approached me as I was walking and said hello. It was common for African American students to speak to one another on campus, even if they didn't know one another. She introduced herself as Chan and she asked me if I was ok. Well I wasn't ok and her asking me, allowed me to open up to her and explain my situation. I knew that she was a leader on campus but I hadn't expected her to direct me to the very office and the very administrator that would help prolong my stay in school. Later on throughout my college experience Chandra definitely encouraged me to give back to the community by joining Project: Youth, the same organization that helped me apply to college. I later became a member of Delta Sigma Theta Sorority, Inc. as well. I soon became a leader on campus within my sorority and through mentoring as the student representative for the YWCA of Urbana-Champaign. I graduated from the university with a Bachelor of Science in Chemistry with distinction. I went on to dental school and completed a residency in Pediatric Dentistry. I understand that to whom much is given much is also required and I have carried that sentiment throughout my life and my career. Today that young woman that introduced herself on campus as Chan is Dr. Chandra Gill. I am not at all surprised that this is the calling God has put on her life. He has been preparing her for sometime now. She was a blessing in my life. She is a strong, positive young woman who always challenged me to be better and to give it my all. I love her for that and I am just one of the many people that she has impacted but she always managed to make me feel like I was the only one.

Caprice J. Banks, 29
Born in Chicago, IL
Counseling Psychology, B.S. University of Illinois @ Urbana-Champaign
Educational Studies, M.Ed. University of Illinois @ Chicago
Creative Writing & Black Literature M.F.A. Chicago State University
English Secondary Education w/
Endorsements in Special Education & Psychology
National Lewis University
Occupation: Educator / Author

The most memorable moment of my mentoring relationship with Chandra was frustrating. It was my senior year in college and my decisions had begun to get the best of me. I began to assess my life, which resulted in overwhelming feelings of disappointment and failure. My love relationship was in turmoil and I could not find the strength to move forward. I poured out the pit of my emotions in an email to Chandra and a couple of other wise women that I trusted to help console me. Moments later, the telephone rang. I answered. The voice on the other end repeated some significant words from the e-mail I'd sent and followed it up with a word of advice that initially frustrated me, but ultimately rescued me from the pit I'd crawled into.

> "Stop throwing this pity party...you're better than this...and nobody's at this party but you. I'm not coming to it...so why are you having it?"

I'd known Chandra long enough to know that she wasn't looking for an answer from me; she posed the question to me to get me to think about my situation and the role I played in my state of affairs. Her cacophonous words pierced my very being. I questioned whether or not I needed her in my life as a big sister, a mentor, but I had no strength to fight. I listened, said goodbye and hung up feeling even more defeated than I had before. I needed to sleep this day away. Days passed and those words began to play in my head over and over again. They were louder than the thoughts of failure and defeat, though harsh and abrupt, they were anointed with healing power. It's been ten years and I've never been to that place again.

I once heard that the ground is no place for a champion; I guess Chandra had heard this before as well. Because there I was making a home in the pit when "Chandra the champion" saw in me what I hadn't seen in myself. She spoke death to my defeat and life to the champion in me. I pass the sentiment forward each and every day of my life as a champion.

Lia Michelle Edens, 32
Born in Denver, CO
Finance, BA University of Illinois @ Urbana-Champaign
Occupation: Sales/Medical Representative Forest Labs

From an early age I can always remember wanting an older sister, but God blessed me with an older brother that protected me and helped me grow into the woman I am today. With that said, God also blessed me with the opportunity to meet Dr. Chandra Gill. Through my relationship with Chandra I learned about the unique bond a younger sister can have with an older sister. I met Chandra a few months into my freshmen year at the "Union" which was on the campus of the University of Illinois. Ironically, I met her through one of my best friends who had two biological sisters; yet she was calling Chandra her big sister when she introduced me to Dr. Gill. I remember saying to my friend why do you need another sister? Her response was simple "Chandra is cool, intelligent, approachable, and a Delta" – this was unusual for an upperclassman to be this down to earth. My friend would say, "I'm her little sister". I soon realized through my interaction with Chandra that I considered her to be my big sister and mentor too. Overtime I saw the guidance and impact Chandra had on other young ladies on and around the campus. She helped counsel me through difficult times in my personal life allowing me to open up about my deepest secrets and fears. The same goes for encouraging me to stay focused on my classes, but also stressing the importance of finding the time to give back to the local community. She helped me grow spiritually. We witnessed to one another God's awesome favor and promises. Chandra also introduced me to many other students like myself that wanted to make a difference on campus—

working through organizations that promoted higher learning and service. Dr. Gill and I may not have the same DNA, but I will always think of her as my big sister.